CONFESSIONS
OF AN
ABANDONED CHILD

BY CURTRINA PHARR

Copyright 2014 by Curtrina Pharr

Published by SPARK Publications
Design and production by SPARK Publications
www.SPARKpublications.com

Cover photo by Deborah Triplett Studios

All rights reserved.

No part of this book may be reproduced, stored in a retrieval system, or transmitted by any means without the written permission of the publisher. The scanning, uploading and distribution of this book via the Internet without the written permission of the publisher is prohibited. Your support of the author's rights is appreciated.

Printing History
Edition One, September 2014

ISBN-10: 0985407085
ISBN-13: 978-0-9854070-8-7

Confessions of an Abondoned Child
by Curtrina Pharr

Throughout this book the names of some places and individuals have been changed.

DEDICATION

I dedicate this book to all the abused and neglected children who feel they have no one to talk to.

ENDORSEMENTS

"When I read her story I thought of Isaiah 40:29-30: 'He gives strength to the weary and increases the power of the weak. Even youths grow tired and weary.' Trina had every reason to be weary with the life she had been dealt, yet God gave her the strength to survive so she could inspire others."
–Valerie Stepp, community volunteer and tax manager at BDO LLP

"Some of the segments punched me in the gut—took my breath away. These are neighbors of mine, not too far away from me, but they could be living in another country far from the one I know. Curtrina's matter-of-fact telling, as though this is nothing unusual, gives the telling tremendous power."
–Jerry Jernigan, Charlotte-based attorney

"*Confessions of an Abandoned Child* brought me to tears and then surprised me with a smile. Curtrina Pharr's raw words pound the experiences of her abusive childhood right into your heart, yet you also see glimpses of happiness and a tinge of hope tucked deep inside her. This book is a must-read for anyone who wants to see change in the world. Curtrina reminds us we can make a difference with our words ... just as she has with hers."
–Liz Neely Heafner, former magazine publisher and Charlotte resident

PREFACE

My hope is this book will expose the abuse, neglect, and failure of the system to provide protection from abusive families. Many families need intervention, and many children need rescue. May this book show readers how little it takes to make a huge difference in a child's life. An encouraging word from you may be remembered for a lifetime.

In writing this book and working with my editors, I attempted to present my reality without describing it in overly graphic or offensive detail. But my reality was offensive to me and should be to you too. So I've left in some of the abusive and street language in direct quotes. I hope you can forgive the foul language, as I forgive those who spoke those words, and God forgives us all.

Acknowledgements

I have many people to thank and acknowledge for their help bringing this book and its message to the world.

First and foremost, this book may not have been written without Catherine Fleming's friendship, support, and connections. She's been with me every step of the way since our first discussion about my journal. We met almost every Saturday for nine months transforming my journal into this book. I learned later that "Miss Catherine" was involved with my family in many ways while she worked for Seeds of Hope at Christ Episcopal Church.

Then through a mutual friend, Catherine met and introduced me to Fabi Preslar who believes in the transformative power of a strong community. Fabi introduced me to a whole team of amazing women who have invested their talents in me so that I can share my story.

Fabi Preslar, her team at SPARK Publications (sparkpublications.com), and my editors, Wendy Gill and Melisa LaVergne, cleaned up my copy. Then her creative team designed the cover and interior pages, and handled printing and production. SPARK Publications is a design firm that specializes in custom publishing and promoting magazines, catalogs, and books.

Deborah Triplett from Deborah Triplett Studios (deborahtriplett.com) captured the cover image and my publicity headshot. Deborah is one of Charlotte's finest photographers, and I feel so blessed by her talent.

Kymm McLean from Who's the Fairest? (whosthefairest.biz) did my hair and makeup for the photo shoot with Deborah. Who's The Fairest? is an agency of beauty professionals specializing in special occasions, weddings, print, and film.

Lou Solomon from Interact (interactauthentically.com) coached me on sharing my story and engaging with a live audience. Interact offers team, group, and individual counseling on communicating authentically.

And finally, I would not be here without Officer Linda, Rock, my brothers and sisters, my nieces and nephews, and other friends and family who have supported, encouraged, and loved me over the years.

Thanks, blessings, and love to you all.

CONTENTS

1: Mama 12	23: Phaze 59
2: Daddy 15	24: D'ajah 60
3: The 'Hood 18	25: April 12, 2000 61
4: James 21	26: Booger 62
5: Aunt Dor'ann 24	27: Motel 6 66
6: Reverend & Sister Crawford 26	28: Dealing 68
	29: Homeless 70
7: May 7, 1994 28	30: Thug Passion 71
8: Nell 31	31: April 3, 2002 72
9: Diamond 34	32: Mr. Lame 78
10: Isis 36	33: April 22, 2002 80
11: Miss Catherine 39	34: Officer Linda 81
12: Big Titty T 42	35: Diamond's Mama 83
13: Sugar Pop 43	36: Mann 85
14: Ms. Palichat 44	37: Abandoned House 87
15: Sheeba 45	38: Rock 90
16: Red 46	39: Net 91
17: Granddaddy Pharr 47	40: Job Corps 93
18: Curtis 49	41: Beautiful Disaster 100
19: Shavonta 50	42: Dwane 102
20: More Aunt Dor'ann 53	43: June 30, 2009 104
21: The Jungle 55	44: Survival 105
22: Storm 56	45: God 107

46: Lessons Learned 109

Miss Trina 110	Red 119
Mama 112	Mann 120
Nell 113	Diamond 122
Booger 115	Officer Linda 123
Shavonta 117	Rock 124

Afterward 126
Meet Curtrina 128

MAMA

1 My mama was beautiful. Her name was Robin Pharr. She had a big, full smile. She used to play in the water hose with us and throw pots of water on us when it was hot outside. Every week we played a card game called Pitty Pat. One time when I was playing Pitty Pat with Mama, she said that if she died she would come back as my sister, not my mama. That made me sad because I wanted a mama.

I remember Mama's smile, and I remember the kind of liquor and beer she drank: it was E & J and Old English 800—the 40-ounce beer. My mama stayed drunk and high on weed.

I guess our mama did the best she could with the five of us kids. She loved us and showed it by fighting for us. She fought the school bus monitor, a kid in the neighborhood, and anybody who messed with us. One time she hit this lady with a broom who had chased me trying to hit me with a broom.

I loved her; she let me whoop my brothers and sisters. It was a reward for the good child to get to beat the other kids in our family. Mama would hold them and let me beat them. She let me get away with a lot of things too. Mama was cool that way.

Mama had five children: Maria, Shavonta (sometimes Shavon for short), Boris, me, and Curtis. Maria was the oldest. Her daddy was Richard, but he never came around much. Maria had beautiful brown skin and perfect teeth.

Her nickname was "Wookie." Nobody ever knew where that nickname came from. She put up with a lot from Mama. Wookie had to feed us, bathe us, do our hair, and get us ready for school. If she didn't do everything just right, Mama would whoop her with a belt. That may be why Wookie told me later that Mama was a very mean woman.

I always looked up to Shavonta. Mama said Shavonta's daddy was a man named Joe, who had dark skin like Shavonta. Other people said Shavonta's daddy was a man named Ray. I've never seen Ray, but they say Shavonta looked just like him. Shavonta didn't take nothing off of nobody. They say one of Mama's boyfriends molested Shavonta, but I don't know if that is true.

Boris was the oldest boy. He was a handsome boy—a ladies' man even back then. When it came to fighting, my brother was talented. He was bossy and controlling, but he protected

> *"Mama was cool that way."*

our family. Mama called Boris "Red" because his skin was lighter and a little red. Maybe his skin color came from my grandfather, Joe Louis Pharr; Mama's daddy was a Cherokee. Red met his daddy once. I will tell you about that later.

And then came me, Curtrina, or Trina to my friends and family. I was born on May 28, 1985. I always copied Shavonta and Red because they got respect. Kids in our neighborhood wouldn't bully Shavonta and Red, because they were afraid of them. When Shavonta and Red told me to fight, I would because I was afraid of them too. But most times I was more like the sweet, shy type who was afraid to say what I was thinking.

Curtis was the youngest. Curtis was very shy, but funny when he did talk. Curtis and I had the same daddy. Our daddy would come and get us and play with us. He did not hurt us, and neither did his mama, Grandma Elizabeth. I protected my brother Curtis because he had a disability: his right hand was a lot smaller than the left. It probably came from my mama's drinking or my daddy's crack cocaine use.

Curtis and I talked about running away to live with our daddy's family. They weren't perfect, but they were hundred times better than living with my mama.

DADDY

2 My daddy's name was Curtis Bay Steele. He was a pimp in the 70s and 80s. He worked at regular jobs too, but he was a pimp for extra money. That's what my aunts told us. Everybody called him "Bay the Butcher" because he would cut any man or woman who crossed him.

Daddy loved my little brother, Curtis, and me. Daddy was what people would call a "street nigga." He hustled to take care of his kids. I thought he was a king because of the way people acted when he came around; he made people nervous. Life was a lot better when Daddy was around.

I remember him driving a sky-blue pickup truck. He parked it on the front lawn by the tree. One time, Mama put me on the back of it and started talking to Daddy at his window. When they were done talking, Daddy pulled off slow and I fell off and scraped my left pinky finger. Mama and Daddy screamed so loud it scared me, and I cried. Daddy picked me up and held me tight and said he was sorry over and over again. He put me on the passenger side and fastened my seat belt and cursed Mama out for putting me on the back of the truck.

Daddy always had a lot of women around. Mama didn't like that. He took me with him to go see a white lady he was dating. She hugged me and played with me. I liked her, so I told mama about the nice lady Daddy let me play with. Mama found the lady and beat her up. Mama was in love with Daddy, but Daddy was in love with the white lady. He married her. Daddy didn't let Mama acting crazy stop him from being in our lives; he still came to get us and would stop by just to play with us.

Daddy was the only one of the guys that Mama made babies with that stuck around for his two kids; he spent time with Mama's other three kids too.

He used to make my sisters and brothers fight over cookies and candy. He only did this when my mama left him to watch all five of us. He liked seeing Shavonta and Red go at it. Wookie always got beat up. Of course, couldn't nobody touch Curtis and me; we got anything we wanted.

Curtis and I picked up our special walks from Daddy. His walk was more like gliding; he folded his middle and ring fingers and kept the other ones straight.

> "Mama was in love with Daddy, but Daddy was in love with the white lady."

My daddy always dressed nice too. He always wore his Afro picked out with either a toothpick or a joint of weed.

Daddy died when I was three and a half years old. My mama took my little brother and me to Daddy's funeral. I remember feeling confused because I saw all of my aunts and uncles and Grandma Elizabeth, but I didn't see Daddy. Aunt Renee took Curtis and me to the front row with Grandma Elizabeth. I didn't understand why everyone was crying. I wanted my daddy to pick me up and hold me like he always did. I started crying and yelling, "Where my daddy? Where my daddy?"

When we left that place, I never saw my daddy again. I don't remember seeing him in a casket; I was too busy watching my grandma cry. It made me sad to see her hurt.

Grandma Elizabeth kept coming around as long as she could, but then she had a stroke and had to be in a wheelchair. She lost a lot of weight too. When I got old enough to visit her on my own, I did. She couldn't smile at my brother and me like she used to. That made me sad.

I know for a fact that Daddy and Grandma Elizabeth loved my brother and me very much.

THE 'HOOD

3 We lived in the projects called Fairview Homes, off of Oaklawn Avenue, in Charlotte, North Carolina. We called it "the 'hood." The apartments were different colors: some were brick red, some light green, and some a cream color. There were some trees but not much grass. We could see the tall buildings in downtown Charlotte from our house.

Grandma Nell, my mama's mama, had an apartment in the same neighborhood. I remember Nell's apartment; it was a cream-colored building. You walked in at the ground floor. Then you had to go up about fifteen steps, which were hard for us to climb, to get to Nell's living room. Nell lived in the apartment with her boyfriend, Sugar Pop. I remember one time Sugar Pop was drunk, and he fell down all the stairs with my little brother, Curtis, in his arms. That fall knocked out all Curtis's baby teeth. We thought that boy was never gonna grow his teeth back. It was a bloody mess.

Nell and Sugar Pop drank a lot. They drank almost every day. There were red and white chitlin buckets beside their beds. Chitlins are pigs' intestines. After Nell and Sugar Pop ate the chitlins, my little brother and I cleaned the buckets so Nell and Sugar Pop could use them to throw up in after they got drunk. The part I hated the most was picking up a bucket full of throw-up. I was little—when I walked, the throw-up would splash on my arms, my face, and my eyes. Nell didn't let us little kids take a bath when we wanted. If my little brother and I did try to clean up, we would listen for Nell's quick steps. If I heard Nell's steps, we would think, "We fixin' to get a whoopin'."

My mama would leave us at my Grandma Nell's apartment to go to the liquor house down the road on Wyatt Street. My mama loved to have fun with her friends. There was always something going on at our house: sex, drugs, screaming, fighting. Curtis and I thought this was funny. We would watch and laugh when Mama and her friends got drunk and do a dance called the Cootie Roll. They would grab between their legs and roll their hips with their tongues sticking out.

Mama was a loyal customer at the liquor house on Wyatt Street. The liquor house was one side of a brick duplex. The other side was the drug house. We knew that because the man

"I wondered why Mama didn't get the grass off the ground."

in the drug house gave us dollar bills. Mama got grass from him. I wondered why Mama didn't get the grass off the ground.

One time, when I was too little to go to school, Mama and I were at the liquor house. I was on a blue flowered mattress that was sort of shiny and satiny. I remember the pillow smelled like throw-up. There was a man on top of my mama. I was crying. I heard Mama yelling. I cried for her. She turned toward me, and said, "Shut the fuck up. I got to get money for y'all to eat."

Every room in the liquor house was very dark and smoky. I was scared someone would try to touch me. I saw people getting touched. There was one light in the kitchen. I remember a man touching an old lady's titties. They were long and skinny titties with big black circles. The man and woman both looked at me and kept on doing what they were doing. It was like I wasn't there.

> *"It was like I wasn't there."*

JAMES

4 Mama started dating James Black, the owner of the liquor house. He was big and tall and had a Jheri curl hairstyle. It made him look like Arsenio Hall in the movie *Coming to America*. He was missing both teeth in the front, but he had a big smile anyway.

We liked James Black. He never beat us or yelled at us. He fixed us cornflakes for breakfast. If we didn't have sugar, he would chop up bananas and put them in our cereal. We all loved it, except for my brother Red. He don't like bananas; he eats his cereal plain.

And James could sing. We loved to hear him sing "Silent Night" by the Temptations. That was Mama's favorite song.

One day Mama and James told us that we were moving to another 'hood called Dellihay Courts. This apartment was a lot bigger with four bedrooms and one and a half baths. We had a playroom downstairs with two blue mattresses for us to jump and wrestle on. My brother Red did back flips on the mattresses. He taught me how to do back flips too.

James used to make us snow ice cream every time it snowed. He said, "We gotta make sure we get the first snow so our ice cream taste fresh." So we all stayed up late to watch James make the ice cream. When the snow got high enough, we all grabbed our coats and hats and put on socks for mittens. Even Mama went outside to gather snow for the ice cream.

We made snow angels and threw snowballs at each other. The socks got wet quick. We went back inside with our fresh snow. We watched James make ice cream in a medium-sized pot; he mixed vanilla flavor in it. We were all happy that night. It was the best ice cream I ever tasted.

James prayed with us too. He told us stories from the Bible. Our favorite story was the story of Samson. James would say that he was Samson, the strongest man in the world. He would flex his muscles and tell all five of us to grab a hold and see if we could pull him down. Of course we never could.

James Black was a hustler. He sold watermelons and liquor to support our family. My brother Red and I loved to help James with the watermelons. James would bring home the watermelons that did not sell. We would line up behind his truck and take one watermelon at a time into

> "It was the best ice cream I ever tasted."

the apartment until his truck was empty. The watermelons stayed on our kitchen floor until the next day. Then James would get us to load them all back on the truck to sell.

James kept lots of guns in Mama's closet. They were big rifles. One day I heard all this screaming and arguing. James had shoved Mama's head outside the upstairs window. I believe James found out about Mama messing with some other man. Mama always told us she would kill us if we told James. That is why I never said anything. We were very sad to see James leave us.

After James left, the Department of Social Services (or DSS) became a part of our family. My daddy's mama, Grandma Elizabeth, called them all the time. But my Mama told us stories about foster homes and how they beat you and lock you up. We always cried when we saw DSS coming, but they never took us away. We were programmed to run and hide from DSS when they came. Even if they talked to me at school, I would lie like crazy because Mama and Nell and Granddaddy Joe said they would beat us if we told the truth. I guess Social Services believed my mama when she said everything was okay.

Aunt Dor'ann

5 Aunt Dor'ann was my mama's sister. She was known for cutting people with knives or glass bottles. One day, she and Mama were sitting at the kitchen table.

Mama said, "Girl, I can't figure out how to feed these chaps."

Then Aunt Dor'ann said, "What you mean, you can't feed these chaps?" Aunt Dor'ann opened the refrigerator. It was empty—nothing. Zero.

Aunt Dor'ann said, "We got to feed 'em."

They went upstairs and got some guns. Mama told Wookie to watch the kids while they were gone. Mama and Aunt Dor'ann went to the neighborhood store. When they came home, they had baloney, bread, and cheese. We had baloney sandwiches with cheese for supper. Mama and Dor'ann started laughing and saying that Mama was going to jail for robbing the store. Mama said, "Bitch, please. Yo' ass goin' to jail!"

That night there was this big loud knock at the door. My mama jumped up and told us all to be quiet. She peeped out the window and saw it was the cops. She told us to get in the closet and keep our mouths shut. So we all got in the hall closet. The cops were all around our apartment.

Mama answered the door. The cop said, "Dor'ann Pharr?" Mama said, "No, I don't know her. My name is Sister." The cop said they were looking for a robbery suspect. The police left. Later that night, Aunt Dor'ann came to our house. Mama told her the police were looking for her. Aunt Dor'ann said, "Fuck them pigs." Both Mama and Dor'ann said they would do it again if it meant feeding us. That showed us that Mama and Aunt Dor'ann really loved us.

Later that week, Aunt Dor'ann got arrested for smoking crack in the park. I asked Mama if Aunt Dor'ann was gone forever. Mama said, "No, baby, just for a little while." Then she told me to go to sleep.

Dor'ann was crazy, but I always loved her.

> *"Later that week, Aunt Dor'ann got arrested for smoking crack in the park."*

REVEREND & SISTER CRAWFORD

6 Mama told us to go to Wilson Heights Church of God on Sunday mornings. Our neighbor Miss Betty talked to Mama about going to church too. But Mama only went to church on Easter to see us in Easter skits and to eat all the food that was there for the Easter celebration.

We met Reverend Crawford at Wilson Heights Church of God. Reverend Crawford always put us in the front row so my brother Red would stay awake. Sister Crawford, the Reverend's wife, was beautiful. She wore two-piece suits—the baby blue suit was the one I liked best. Sister Crawford's skirts were tight around the knees.

One day I was dressed in an all-white dress. I balled my dress up in the back so it would be tight like Sister Crawford's. Fixing my dress like that made Sister Crawford laugh. When she laughed, she hugged me and made me feel like she loved me. Every Sunday I got to sit with Sister Crawford in the choir. I felt happy. I wanted to be like the Crawfords. They were happy people who did not fight and shout and say they were going to kill somebody.

Reverend Crawford said that if you believed in Jesus, things would get better. The Wilson Heights church gave us some clothes and shoes. (My mama didn't like shoes and never wore them.) The church fed us too. I liked believing things could get better.

Didn't seem like anyone or anything could make things better the day Mama died though.

> "When she laughed, she hugged me and made me feel like she loved me."

MAY 7, 1994

7 We were all sitting in the living room downstairs watching Bugs Bunny. My oldest sister, Wookie, was washing clothes. My mama got up to go upstairs. I ran after her; I was always hanging on her. She started going up the steps. Then she squatted down. She kissed me on the forehead and said, "Go back downstairs, baby." So I did.

Red, Curtis, and I were on the floor watching Bugs Bunny. Shavonta was stretched out on the couch. Wookie was washing clothes and getting everything ready for us to go to school the next day.

Wookie yelled up, "Mama, do you want me to hang out the clothes?" No answer. Wookie yelled up again, "MAMA, do you want me to hang out the clothes?" Then she yelled it one more time. Then Wookie ran up the stairs.

We heard a loud scream, and Wookie was at the top of the steps screaming, "Y'all, Mama's dead! Mama's dead!"

Red, who always had an attitude, said, "Wookie, if you lying, I'ma beat your ass." He was just nine, but he was the man of the family.

I ran up the stairs to my mama's room. She was on the floor with a deck of cards lying all around her. Curtis and I started crying and begging her to wake up. The ambulance came and took my mama away. I didn't know why my mama didn't come back.

The next time I saw her, Mama was in a white casket with a white dress on. Wookie picked me up so I could see her.

I touched her. "She don't feel like Mama," I said.

Wookie said, "Well it is her."

"Why she so hard? Why she so cold?" I asked.

Wookie said, like I should know, "She dead. She ain't comin' back."

Shavonta was crying, and she told me, "Mama is in heaven."

Another thing happened at Mama's funeral. My brother Red saw his father for the first time.

Red always said he wanted to see his daddy. Well his daddy came to Mama's funeral. I hid behind a tree in our front yard so I could see Red's daddy. My mama's brother, Harry Pharr, said, "That's your daddy right there, boy," pointing to this big guy named Mac. Red looked at Uncle Harry and then he looked at Mac. Red looked excited, like he was about to get a present.

> *"Nobody ever talked about Mama. She died, and that was it."*

Mac looked back at Red. Then he laughed and said, "Don't neva' call me Daddy. I ain't your daddy." Red's face changed real quick. He ran into the house, and I ran after him. He breathed real hard. I ain't never seen Red cry so much. Then he went to the monkey bars and beat up a little girl named Angela.

Mama died the day before Mother's Day. The night before she died, I gave her a golden egg I made at school for Mother's Day. She was drunk and having a seizure on the living room couch. Her eyes would cross when she had a seizure. But my Mama said the egg was pretty and she loved it. That made me happy. Then she asked me what kind of cake I wanted for my birthday in a couple of weeks. I said that I wanted a Rapunzel cake.

I knew about Rapunzel from story time at school. She was a girl who was locked up, but someone came to save her. I liked to pretend I was Rapunzel. I would put a long bath towel on my head and spin around in circles saying, "Rapunzel, Rapunzel, let down your hair!" (I always said this in a really soft voice because I was scared that I would get in trouble if I talked loud enough for someone to hear me.)

Two weeks after my mama died, I turned nine years old. Nell asked me what kind of birthday cake I wanted. I told her I wanted a chocolate cake with a picture of Rapunzel with long, pretty hair. She said she would try to find one. But Nell was old; she didn't know nothing about Rapunzel. She gave me a pink hair scrunchy with colorful beads. It was the only birthday present I got that year.

Nobody ever talked about Mama. She died, and that was it. Nobody else talked about my birthday either. We didn't talk much in my family.

NELL

8 Sometime after Mama died, Nell, Sugar Pop, and us five kids moved into a house in North Charlotte on North Caldwell Street. The neighborhood was called Optimist Park, but I'm not sure why it was called this. The house that Nell rented was brown and had brown shutters. It had a porch with brown posts holding the roof up. It used to be two houses, but now it was one house with four bedrooms and two bathrooms. It was the biggest house we had ever seen. Shavonta, Wookie, and I shared a room.

There was no grass in the yard, only rocks. Nell planted a little tomato garden to the side of the porch with about six plants. From our front yard you could see the tall buildings in downtown Charlotte. The only time I had ever been downtown was when I ate at McDonalds after Mama took me to get shots. The buildings were a way for me to know where our street was if I got lost walking back to Caldwell Street. On the Fourth of July, we could see the fireworks going off from the tall buildings.

There was a church across the street from Nell's house with a park behind it where we would play some when Nell passed out. Curtis and I were not allowed out of the house, so we had to wait until Nell went to sleep from drinking too much. Nell drank vodka in a bottle with a red label. She chased it with water.

When we moved into the brown house on Caldwell Street, Nell told us, "Disrespect me, and you will get yo' ass tore up just like your mama did when I raised her." One day I had on a pair of Daisy Duke shorts with a yellow lion on the back pocket. They were real short shorts. My grandma said, "What the hell you got on? Go take that damn shit off." I started stomping my feet, and then I said, "I don't like you!"

My grandma turned and looked at me with a mean stare. Her eyes were like slits. In a calm, scary whisper she asked, "What you say to me?"

I didn't say a word. She told me not to move. She went to the bathroom and started filling the tub with water. She told me to take off all of my clothes and get in the tub. I stood in the tub naked and scared.

She left the room and came back with three long hickory sticks. I saw her do this many times later on. The switches were about six feet long. She got me to hold the big end of the stick while I stood in the bathtub. She braided three sticks together. She rubbed alcohol on those sticks. She never took her eyes off of me. I started shaking. Nell told me to let go of the sticks so she could hold the big end.

She stood in the bathroom doorway and started beating me. I heard those sticks swish through the air, and then they slapped my skin. I could not stand up in the tub and started slipping trying to get away from the sticks.

Then Nell told me to get out of the tub and face the wall behind the tub. I heard the swish and felt the sting. She started whipping me over and over with that stick. She was yelling at me while she whipped me on my back; then she whipped me on my legs. "I didn't let yo' mama disrespect me. And y'all ain't either. If you EVER raise your voice again to me little girl, I kill ya'! Now get your fast ass in that room and stand in the middle of the floor 'til I get in there." Fast is what my grandmother called promiscuous girls.

My brothers and sisters were watching and listening. Nell looked at them and proudly raised the braided sticks. She strutted down the hallway yelling, "Which one of y'all wants some? Disrespect me? I ain't your mama; I'm yo' grandma. Yo' mama's mama. You will get what she got. Now go to bed!"

They all took off running to their rooms. Even Red was scared. I had never seen Red scared before, so I knew Nell wasn't no joke. Don't mess with Grandma; Grandma whoop you.

Then Nell came back in the room with me. I was naked and scared and thinking I was gonna get more. But now she was calm. She picked up a bottle of rubbing alcohol and said, "Come here, girl."

She began rubbing the alcohol on the welts forming on my body. It stung but not half as bad as the switch. "Baby, I loved your mama, but I be damned if I was gonna let you think that it would be okay for you to raise your voice at me or any other adult. I knew one of y'all was gonna be an example and buck at me, but I didn't think it'd be your lil' ass. I thought it would be that damn Red." She put my night-clothes on and kissed me and told me she loved me. She reminded me of my mama like that. Mama used to always tell me she loved me after she beat me.

You know something funny? I thought my grandma put alcohol on those sticks to get the germs off them. It made me think about how she really did care about me. But then somebody told me she put that alcohol on the sticks to make them sting more when they cut my skin.

DIAMOND

9 One good thing that happened on Caldwell Street was that I met my best friend Diamond. We were in the fourth grade together. Diamond lived about seven doors down from our brown house with her mother. It was nice and peaceful at Diamond's house.

Diamond was popular. She was the funny type too. I was always the quiet one doing the laughing but not the joke maker. If we started in the same class at the beginning of the year, we were split up right away because Diamond and I always got into some kind of trouble. My little brother always tagged along with Diamond and me.

I had other friends in Optimist Park. Sarah was tall and skinny like Olive Oil on Popeye; she even walked like Olive Oil with her arms swinging and wobbling. Sarah couldn't be still for nothing.

And then there was Tonya, who always made me laugh. She loved to do baby dolls' hair and draw pictures of different hairstyles; she was pretty good. One time Tonya's mama, Bev, had a birthday party for Tonya at the Trade Winds Skating Rink on Central Avenue. I wanted to go so bad, but Nell would never let Curtis or me go out of the house. Tonya's mama even came to our house and asked Nell if I could come to Tonya's birthday. Nell said, "Hell no," and slammed the door. I cried.

But my best friend was Diamond. Diamond was very smart, especially in math. Diamond said she wanted to be a lawyer.

Diamond and I would compete to see who could make the most As. Diamond always made straight As.

One day I found out that I made the A/B Honor Roll. I was excited to tell Nell and ran into the house. "Nell—look, look!" I shouted. But I didn't hear nothing, so I went into the back room where Nell watched TV. She was asleep on the couch with a pint of liquor on her chest. I put my book bag down, went out, and shut the door.

I went to the park behind the church. Diamond and Tonya were there trying to do splits. I knew how to do a split because I used to be on a step team, the Kids Against Violence Steppers. I even won a dance contest by doing a full split and then lying flat on my stomach; it was called doing the Cry Baby. Tonya tried to do a split, but she could not get all the way down. I told her to stand up and go as far down as she could. All of a sudden, Diamond kicked Tonya's inside ankle out. Tonya fell to a full split and peed all over herself! She went home crying. Diamond and I laughed about that.

Then Diamond said that we should try to smoke. Diamond got some notebook paper and pulled up some old grass from the ground. She told me to get a lighter or some matches from my house, so I did. Diamond and I went to the back of the park and tried to light it, but it wouldn't light. Finally Diamond got it lit and passed it to me. I didn't know what we were doing, but I pretended to smoke it anyway. Then Diamond and I pretended we were high. We did back flips off the swings and swung around and around until we were "drunk."

The streetlights came on, so we knew that it was time for us to get home. When I went inside, Nell was still passed out.

Diamond and I were like sisters, and her mama was the closest thing to a mama that I ever had.

ISIS

10 I wanted to be treated better at home. I wanted to be happy and free. Nell made us feel like prisoners because we had to stay in the house all day. It was boring when there was nothing going on. Nell made us watch cooking and fishing shows.

My cousin Isis lived down the street. Things were not good at her house either. Isis and I always talked about running away to go live with Aunt Leanne, who was Nell's younger sister. My cousin and I were in fifth grade at Winding Springs Elementary School together. One day, we decided to go to the counselor and tell her everything that was happening at home. We thought we could get moved to Aunt Leanne's if we told about the alcohol and the beatings.

Things did not turn out like we thought they would. When we got off the school bus that afternoon, Nell was standing behind the screen door with her hands on her hips. She had that look on her face that said a whipping was coming. We walked toward the house. Nell opened the door, and Isis's mama busted out the door and said, "Bitch, you better take your ass home. I'm gonna beat the shit out of you. You already know what time it is."

Isis took off running to her house crying. She knew what was coming.

Nell looked at me and said, "Come on. Come on."

When I walked in the house, my cousin Booger was

there and Aunt Leanne and some other cousins. Booger said, "You been down at that school house tellin' about your grandma business? Well you know if them people call Social Services, they gonna put y'all in a foster home. You know what they do in them foster homes, don't you?"

I shook my head no. Booger kept on. "Well you could get raped, or they treat you like a slave. They don't care about your ass at that schoolhouse. Nobody care about your ass."

Nell blurted out, "My sister don't want your ass. Go on into the back bathroom and take your clothes off." I walked real slow and cried the whole way.

I went to the bathroom and took off all my clothes like Nell said. Nell came in with a long, thick, black belt. She held the buckle part and started swinging.

"Didn't I tell you not to go to that damn schoolhouse telling my damn business?" I felt the belt sting like alcohol on an open cut. I used my arms to protect myself, but the belt slammed on against my back and legs over and over again. Nell screamed, "Where they at now? Can they come save you now?" It seemed like nobody could save me.

> *"Nell had tried to make sure the welts were on my back and the top of my legs where people wouldn't see."*

Nell kept swinging and said, "When you go back to that school Monday morning, you better tell them you lied."

Monday morning Nell dressed me in pants and a thick, long sleeved shirt that was too hot for the day. Nell had tried to make sure the welts were on my back and the top of my legs where people wouldn't see. But when she hit me, I was swinging my arms, so Nell hit my arms too. The belt left wide, red lines where it hit. Those belt marks looked like train tracks on my legs and arms, all crisscrossed and going in all directions.

When Isis came to school, she had black eyes and red marks like she had been kicked. She had welts with cuts in them too, but they looked different from my welts. Isis was mixed, so the beating showed on her skin more than mine. The school bus driver took Isis to the office. They called me in to the office. When Isis saw me, she ran up and hugged me and said, "I don't want to go home. I'm scared. Trina, tell these people that my mama beat me all the time."

I was too scared to say anything. We cried. They asked me questions, and I lied like I'd been told to. I said that I made it all up because I was mad at my grandma.

Isis did not go back home. She got sent to Aunt Leanne's. I thought Aunt Leanne didn't want me because Isis was prettier than I was.

I learned my lesson. I never told nobody nothing again (until now). It didn't matter what Reverend Crawford had said; I wasn't going to get help from Jesus or anybody else.

MISS CATHERINE

11 Nell let us go to the after-school program at the church. Miss Beverly was one of our teachers. She had false teeth. She would help me with my homework and tap her pencil, saying, "You can do this, Trina. You can do this." Diamond would lean over and whisper, "Trina, make her say it again. Her teeth gonna fall out!"

When I was in the fifth grade, I met a lady named Miss Catherine at the church. I had seen her in the 'hood. She worked to get people to the doctor or other things they needed. She had red-blonde hair like gold. Reverend Crawford used to say that heaven had gold streets, and her hair reminded me of that. She came up to me and said, "Hi, my name is Catherine. Who are you?"

Miss Catherine was the first real person I met who looked happy. She had a big smile and she was always glad to see me.

I had seen happy people like Miss Catherine on *Family Matters* and *The Cosby Show*. I would watch those shows and wish I was happy like that. I wanted to be like Rudy on *The Cosby Show* because everybody loved her. But I was not like Rudy. Most of the time, I was afraid of what might happen next. Mainly, I was afraid of two things: getting raped and not having something to eat.

I did not know for sure why Miss Catherine was in the 'hood, but I liked being with her. She told me that someday things would get much better.

Miss Catherine tried to get me help through a therapist. She thought something was going on deep inside me, but she couldn't get me to talk about it. The therapist couldn't either. I was fed up with getting in trouble for talking too much. I was done with talking.

But one day I did tell Miss Catherine that I felt ugly. She asked me why I felt ugly. I didn't know what to say. Nobody ever asked me that kind of question before. They would just say, "Shut the hell up and lay down." I told her that I had bumps on my face. I did not know what was happening to my face. I thought pieces of white bone were sticking through my skin.

> "I thought pieces of white bone were sticking through my skin."

Miss Catherine said it was normal to have acne, and we could go see a doctor. We went to a dermatologist and got me some medicine. The medicine worked. I felt beautiful.

One day Miss Catherine talked to us kids about surprising Nell for her birthday by cleaning the house. We were scared about surprising Nell. Miss Catherine planned for someone to take Nell to the beauty parlor to get her hair done and her nails too. As soon as Nell was out of sight, we took everything out of the house and put it in the front yard. We all started cleaning, and Red painted the front porch. Red really painted that porch—the floor and all. Miss Catherine took on the kitchen. When she moved things, the roaches raced up the wall. I moved the dresser in the back room. I moved it by myself. Miss Catherine had a fit when she seen me move that dresser by myself.

When Nell came home she saw that front porch and came flying into the house, screaming "What the fuck y'all doing to my house?" Even Miss Catherine was scared. But then Nell stopped and looked around and saw the living room clean with all the junk put up. She smiled. We told her this was her birthday surprise.

I told Miss Catherine later that the first thing Nell did when Miss Catherine left was go out to the gray trashcan to get her homemade Muscadine wine out of the trash. Miss Catherine didn't know what it was and had thrown it out.

Miss Catherine stopped coming to the church after awhile. I didn't understand why she never came back.

BIG TITTY T

12 We had family all over Caldwell and North Davidson Streets in North Charlotte. We had lots of cousins who came to play with us. Their homes were not too great either.

We had a cousin named Big Titty T. She was fun and loud. She would come to our house and drink and laugh. She was short; she was maybe five feet tall. She had beautiful long black hair. T had titties that touched her knees. For real! That is why she was called Big Titty T. She was always drinking beer. She always put her beer in the microwave. I never knew why; she just liked hot beer.

Sugar Pop was Nell's boyfriend, but Big Titty T would flirt with Sugar Pop. She would put her big titties on top of Sugar Pop's head. Even though Sugar Pop had a big head, those titties would cover his head all up. Nell would get so mad at T. Us kids thought it was funny.

"T had titties that touched her knees."

SUGAR POP

13 We liked messing with Sugar Pop when he was drunk or having a seizure. I think he had seizures because Nell would hit him upside the head with pots, glass ashtrays—whatever was around. His head was real big, so Nell never missed! When Sugar Pop had a seizure, his bottom lip would be real big and hang down; he couldn't talk, and drool would come out of his mouth.

One day we decided to get clippers and cut his hair. It ended up looking like polka dots all over his head. It was a mess. Then we got a red dress with black polka dots from Nell's closet. We put that on Sugar Pop. We found an old wig of Nell's too. We said, "Oooh, Sugar Pop, you look fine." Finally he came out of his seizure, but he was still drunk. Sugar Pop stood up and wiggled his butt like a dog wagging his tale. He let out a laugh like a dry cough that went on and on. Later on, Sugar Pop passed out.

The next day, Nell woke up and saw Sugar Pop lying in their bed with her dress on, and she said, "What you doin' with all my damn clothes on?" Sugar Pop said, "Those chaps must have messed with me while I was asleep."

We had some funny times on Caldwell Street.

MS. PALICHAT

14 I liked school. Even though we were poor, we were popular because we were fun. My favorite subjects were language arts, reading, and writing. I never could shake math.

I especially liked writing stories and poems and rap love songs. I could write down my feelings, and it didn't matter that nobody was listening. I only showed what I wrote to people I trusted.

Ms. Palichat was my sixth grade teacher. She was the first teacher to notice my writing ability. I wrote a story about tornadoes. I named the tornadoes Faldo, Feraldo, and Maldo. Ms. Palichat made me feel proud about that story. The only other time I felt proud was when Mama said I was the best house cleaner.

Ms. Palichat took me shopping and to her house for Christmas. She bought me a black dress with a pink daisy on the front. She gave me black sandals and some thick black tights too. That dress was the prettiest thing I ever owned.

I loved Ms. Palichat.

"I loved Ms. Palichat."

SHEEBA

15 When I was about ten, Nell let us get a puppy. We named the puppy Sheeba. I couldn't wait to see Sheeba when I got out of school. I liked to hug her. Nell even let Sheeba stay in the house for a while. I felt safe with Sheeba near me. Sheeba was tan and white, fluffy, and not very big. She was a happy puppy.

One day, Sheeba got hit by a school bus. Her leg was broken, so I found a stick and some laces from Sugar Pop's shoes and tied the stick to her leg to make it straight. She let me do that to her. It was like she knew I was trying to help her. She did get better for a while.

Then Sheeba got worms and threw up all over the living room floor. Nell said she had to stay outside. I cried because I wanted Sheeba to sleep with me, so we could make each other feel better.

The next day when I woke up, Sheeba was outside dead. It was raining, and I cried and cried. Nell and my cousin laughed at me for crying over a dog. That hurt even more. I rocked myself back and forth and cried and cried.

Snoop was our family dog who did live outside. When Sheeba died, I hugged Snoop around the neck and cried some more. Snoop understood me. I knew Snoop loved me. I stole hotdogs and other food from the kitchen for him, so maybe that is why Snoop loved me.

RED

16 My brother Red liked dogs too. He took good care of them at first, but later he started training dogs to fight.

My brother Red was a talented fighter. I was afraid of him because he would fight anybody. Sometimes my friends and I would be hanging on the block, and someone would spot my brother, and I would hide until he left. I looked up to Red because he had respect from everybody in the neighborhood.

When Curtis got in trouble at school, Red got a little boy Curtis's age to fight Curtis. Red wouldn't let me jump in and help my little brother. I was so pissed! But Curtis didn't come home with bad grades the next semester.

Shavonta was the only one out of the four of us kids that would step up to Red. They used to fight with clothing irons and glass ashtrays.

Red taught me how to take chances. He was strong, and he was daring. He and I liked to jump off of buildings. We jumped off the church, our house on North Caldwell Street, and our cousin Booger's house across the street. I got my brave heart from Red.

Red was a risk taker, and he didn't take nothing off nobody.

GRAND-DADDY PHARR

17 Red did not get along with our mama's daddy, Joe Louis Pharr. After Nell divorced him, Granddaddy remarried a Caucasian lady. He came to our house every Saturday. He bought us one pair of shoes a year. Granddaddy drank Bulls Malt Liquor, and he smoked Camel cigarettes with no filter.

My mama said when she was little Joe Louis would make her, her two brothers, and her sister, Dor'ann, crawl up and down the hallway naked and beat them as they crawled by him. Nell would beat them too.

But Granddaddy never whooped or yelled at me. Granddaddy would not allow anyone to yell at me when he was around; I was his "baby girl." He smiled at me a lot. Granddaddy had a gold tooth on the side of his mouth. I thought that was cool.

Granddaddy bought me lots of things. I was always excited to see him on Saturday. He would come into the house with a case of beer and ask, "Which one been messin' with you, baby girl?" Then he said, "I was chief of a Cherokee tribe. None of these bitches can mess with me."

But I was still afraid of Granddaddy because I saw the way he beat Shavonta and Red.

Everybody changed when Granddaddy came around. I saw him rub on my friends on their breasts and their legs. Sometimes he would pay them for a feel. People said that he slept with some family members, but I do not remember him touching me.

One day Red had enough of Granddaddy beating him, so he stood up to him. Red said, "I am the man."

My granddaddy walked out to his car, popped the trunk, and pulled out a .50 caliber handgun. He said, "This will lay your ass down little boy."

Red took off. Granddaddy said he would shoot Red if he ever caught up with him. Red started training dogs to fight after that.

And when Nell saw Red stand up to Granddaddy, she did not try to discipline Red anymore. If you could stand up to Joe Louis, you sure could stand up to Nell Pharr too.

> "Red started training dogs to fight after that."

CURTIS

18 Curtis could never talk right because all of his teeth had been knocked out when Sugar Pop dropped him.

Nell always dressed Curtis, even when he was nine years old. She dressed him in a batman shirt with a black cape. Nell put him in suspenders with high-water jeans. He had glasses. He looked like Steve Urkel from the *Family Matters* TV show.

By the time Curtis was ten, the teeth that got knocked out were growing back. But it's a wonder they stayed in! Red and everybody in the family and I picked on Curtis.

Everybody at school did too, but we protected Curtis at school. He would cry all the time.

> *"She dressed him in a batman shirt with a black cape."*

SHAVONTA

19 By the time I was eleven years old, us Pharr kids ran Caldwell Street. Shavonta took nothing off of nobody. Shavonta was fun. She was brave. She was PHAT: pretty, hot, and tempting. She knew how to dress. She never dated a broke guy, only successful drug dealers. Shavonta was the boss—always—and of everybody.

Shavonta got raped by one of our cousins when she was nine or ten. After that, Shavonta would fight. Wookie, my oldest sister, got raped by the same guy. But Wookie just got quiet.

I looked up to Shavonta. She fought for me when I needed help in the 'hood, and she had control over her life. I knew not to mess with Shavonta; I knew my limit when teasing her. She didn't take no mess off of me either.

Shavonta was the black sheep of the family. I call her this because she had darker skin than we did. She had nappier hair and got blamed for everything. Shavonta was treated like an animal in our family. My mama and my grandma beat her all the time.

We would always say, "Shavonta did it!" She got beaten with a bat, a pot, whatever. She would take the beatings for us, even when we got older. It was like she built herself up to be beaten— like a fighter. She learned to take it. It was like the beatings were the only thing she could feel. And she got to scream.

Shavonta started drinking when she was eleven or twelve.

She started smoking weed and skipping classes when she was in middle school. By the time she was thirteen, Shavonta was selling crack out of our bedroom window; Nell could hear the door open but not the window.

When Shavonta was fourteen, she started dating a guy in the neighborhood. Everybody called him Lil' Steve because he was short. Lil' Steve had every pair of Air Jordans they made. He dressed nice too, in Tommy Hilfiger shirts and jeans. Shavonta had been flirting with him for a while.

She started sneaking him through our bedroom window. I slept with Wookie in the same room. Lil' Steve was maybe fifteen or sixteen. Shavonta and Lil' Steve started having sex. I think he was her first love. Shavonta would skip school and hang out at Lil' Steve's house.

My grandma Nell had one hand with rings on each finger. She had about three rings per finger, and they were big rings. She would backhand the mess out of Shavonta when she could catch her.

My grandma Nell got threatened with being arrested because Shavonta was skipping school. When Shavonta did go to school, she got suspended on purpose. She had an open case with the social worker. One day Nell called the social worker; they got the cops and went around to Lil' Steve's house. They pulled Shavonta out of that house and took her to a group home. Grandma Nell couldn't handle Shavonta anymore.

I was sad to lose Shavonta, and I was mad at Nell for putting her out. In some ways, Shavonta made me feel safe, and in some ways she scared me because I knew how she could fight.

Without Shavonta, I felt lost. She was my idol. Wookie was not fun, and I would not mess with Red. Curtis was my puppet. So Shavonta was the only person I could tease and have fun with. I was mad at Nell for sending my protector away. I thought Nell should have given her another chance.

But Shavonta kept breaking loose from the group homes and coming back to Caldwell Street. She said that was her home. She couldn't smoke weed at the group home. And she said she couldn't sleep at the group home because she needed to hear sirens and guns shots, and to be in the mix of the hell house. That was what she knew and what she felt safe with. She knew how to survive in the world on Caldwell Street.

Finally, Nell gave up and let Shavonta do what she wanted. And Shavonta sure could raise hell at our house on Caldwell Street. She could raise hell anywhere.

> "... she couldn't sleep at the group home because she needed to hear sirens and guns shots ... "

MORE AUNT DOR'ANN

20 When Aunt Dor'ann came to our house on Caldwell Street, she was almost always high on something. She came to our house real drunk one day. She staggered in the back door and called Shavonta. She knew Shavonta was selling crack out of my grandma's house.

Dor'ann said, "Shavonta, give me a dime until I get my check." A dime is $10 worth of crack, enough for one or two hits.

Shavonta said, "Hell no! Hollah at me when you get your check."

So Dor'ann got mad and started hollering and cursing. Shavonta cursed back. Nell heard all the screaming and said, "Y'all shut that shit up! Dor'ann get the hell out of my house!"

Aunt Dor'ann grabbed a pot and hit Nell upside the head. Nell hit the floor. Nell was down just like Mama was when she died. Shavonta went crazy!

She picked Aunt Dor'ann up and tossed her onto the stove.

Shavonta hit Aunt Dor'ann in the face over and over. And then Shavonta dragged Aunt Dor'ann through the house, out the front door, and over the rocky front yard. One of Nell's cousins came running over. When she heard what happened, she dropped kicked Aunt Dor'ann and stomped her on the ground.

My grandma Nell was fifty-three years old when this happened. She was hurt pretty bad, but she was drunk, so she just laid down and went to sleep. That was the first time I saw Nell get beaten.

The next day everything was back to normal. Aunt Dor'ann came by after her chemotherapy treatment. Aunt Dor'ann's right breast had been removed; she had a fake silicone breast she put in her bra. It felt real. Sometimes she would throw it at us to make us laugh.

Aunt Dor'ann would tell us the funniest stories. She would prostitute herself if she wanted some crack. One night she and this guy were in the woods. It was real, real dark. He undid her bra and felt that there was no breast. Aunt Dor'ann said, "Don't worry, baby. That one gone, but I got the real one right here." She told us she put her real breast in his mouth. He didn't know what was happening, but she got her crack.

I was eleven when Aunt Dor'ann told me that story. But I had already seen it all by then.

THE JUNGLE

21 "The jungle" was what we called the park in our neighborhood. It had a bridge over Little Sugar Creek. There were benches to sit or sleep on. There were lots of trees and pathways to other parts of the park. It was a safe place to hide.

It was the jungle because there were no rules. Crackheads smoked crack there. We drank there. We fought there. We had dogfights there. People had sex for money there.

Now that everyone in our family who abused us was dead or had given up on us, we found other people to abuse. We wanted to fight because we were used to fighting every day. And we won every fight on the streets, so we felt safe, strong, and proud.

We Pharrs owned the jungle. If we did not own the jungle, we would be killed by it.

> *"If we did not own the jungle, we would be killed by it."*

STORM

22 I got kicked out of school for fighting in the seventh grade. They sent me to management school. I was drinking and smoking weed by that time.

That summer I met this girl, Storm, who lived down the street. She was just out of jail and was about twenty-five or twenty-six years old. She was a thick, big girl; she was pretty, but she had a deep voice like a man's. I guess her voice was deep from smoking. She taught me how to dress sexy, how to weave my hair, and how to defend my drug money.

Our day would begin and end with her telling me what to do. Storm gave me a place to live when I was afraid to go home to Nell. She was tough, and she taught me how to use my body to make money.

Storm would use me to get drugs by dressing me up and telling guys they could look but not touch. I was her property. She used me to attract guys who would buy sex from her.

To make it easier, I got high when we went out on the streets, but I was still scared. I just let them look; there was no sex. I belonged to Storm. I was the "do girl" for her whole family. Whatever they told me to do, I did. In return, I had a roof over my head. Her mama even told me to get out there and bring in some money.

By now, I was in the eighth grade. The last day I went to

Eastway Middle School was with Storm. She dressed me in a red, tight, spandex dress. It stretched to my knees, but Storm said, "Nah bitch; pull it up." We smoked some weed and drank Natural Ice beer. We drove into Eastway Middle School with the music bumping.

Storm told me to go into the school to get my things out of my locker. The security guard saw me coming into the entrance with my dress pulled up and my body on display, but she didn't say nothing.

I was too mature for school anyway. I had enough of all the rules and people pretending like they cared. Every time I told them about what was going on in my life, it always backfired. I had nothing to lose.

I cleaned out my locker. Diamond came up. "What the fuck are you doing?"

I said, "Cleaning out my locker."

Diamond was surprised and said, "You dropping out of school?"

"Yeah."

"Who brought you here?"

"Storm," I said.

Diamond looked at me like I was a fool. "You're a stupid bitch." And we were not close friends after that, at least for a while.

> *"She taught me how to dress sexy, how to weave my hair, and how to defend my drug money."*

That same day, Storm and I went back to North Charlotte to return her cousin's car to him. He was a 'hood superstar who had kilos of crack. He was the man, the boss. He gave us some weed to smoke. He gave us crack to go sell in the jungle. Storm and I got high on weed and liquor.

Storm and I went to her cousin's house. There were some men there. There was lots of liquor there. There was weed too. I remember dancing and then throwing up on the porch; I don't know how we made it back to the 'hood.

The next day, Shavonta and I walked to the Giant Penny Grocery to steal some food. We went into the store to look around, and this dude kept following us from aisle to aisle.

Shavonta finally turned on him and said, "What the fuck you keep followin' us for?"

He looked straight at me and said, "Baby girl. You don't remember me from last night?"

I said, "No, I was drunk as hell."

He said, "That girl Storm did you dirty last night, and my boy got it on tape." He said the tape was at his house behind the store.

Shavonta said, "Come on. Let's go see what he got."

The video showed Storm and me partying. There were these two guys. They were fat and old with spiky grey beards. The video showed me drunk out of my mind, rapping with Storm. Then it showed me passed out on a chair.

The tape cut off for a while. When it came back on, Storm was naked. She lifted my arm up, looked at the camera, and let my arm flop back down. Then she spread my legs.

All my life I was afraid of being raped by a man; I never thought about being raped by a woman.

PHAZE

23 Phaze was Shavonta's new boyfriend. He moved into Nell's house.

Phaze was the second most successful drug dealer in our 'hood. He beat Shavonta over and over again for all kinds of things. Phaze beat her for not being able to find his underwear and for losing some of his crack. One time he beat her because he wanted to have sex with her best friend. He beat Shavonta so he could run the street. The fights got worse and worse.

We kids had lived in Nell's house for about five years. Nell let us come and go and do what we wanted. But Nell was scared of abuse from a man. She was so scared of Phaze that she moved out. She took Curtis with her and went to live with one of my cousins.

After that, all hell broke loose.

D'AJAH

24 We turned Nell's brown house on Caldwell Street into a party house, a dog kennel, and a drug house. It was a duplex; Phaze and Shavonta were dealing drugs on one side, and Red kept his dogs on the other side.

Red was making money fighting dogs. Red's dogs ate, slept, and went to the bathroom inside our house. We were afraid to go on that side because the dogs would attack us. Red would box the dogs; they were afraid of him too.

One time I walked over to the side of the house with the dogs. I heard Red say with a snaky sound, "Get her." Snoop started coming at me, and I had to run to get away from him.

Even Snoop, the dog I loved and was my friend, had turned mean. Red had beaten our family dog just like all his other dogs. When you are scared, you fight, or you run if you can get away. Snoop had learned to fight too, just like us.

When Shavonta was seventeen, she got pregnant. Shavonta named her baby girl D'ajah Samone Ma'kya. We were all excited to have someone who would love us and someone we could love. She would love us no matter what.

D'ajah loved me from day one.

April 12, 2000

25 This was the day that Nell died. It was one month before my fifteenth birthday. By this time, I had been to at least five funerals, all of them for family.

The last time I saw Nell was about two weeks before at her sister's house.

I said, "Hi Nelly Poo."

"What your crazy ass been up to?" Nell said. "You better not been out there smoking that dope." She called weed "dope."

I said, "Can I have some of your chicken?"

Nell said, "You sell all of that damn dope, and you can't buy no damn chicken?"

Then she gave me some chicken and hugged me.

"You better take care of yourself 'cause your grandma won't be here forever."

I always felt bad because of the fight I had with Nell when I told her I didn't want to live with her anymore. I cried some when Nell died. Then I went on with my life.

Nell was mean, but she did care about us. Curtis and I got a check from Social Security from when our daddy worked. But Nell did not let us live with her just for the money. Nell really wanted us because we were her grandkids. She loved us in her own way.

BOOGER

26 My cousin Booger also lived across the street from the church, catty-cornered from Nell. After Nell died, Booger snitched to the landlord that us kids were living in the house alone. He kicked us all out for good.

I was sitting on the church steps, thinking. Booger came over. She was drunk, and she said, "Trina, let me hollah at you right quick."

Booger said, "Now your granddaddy asked me if I wanted to take in all you chaps. Now you and Curtis get your daddy's social security checks every month. I don't want you to think that I want you for your check, like your daddy's family does. If you live with me, I will give you your whole check. You don't have to stay in the house; you can do what you want to do. I just want you to have somewhere to stay because I love you. I don't want nothin' to happen to y'all."

The way Booger got Curtis to move in with her was to promise him clothes. Curtis and I had the same father, so we each got a Social Security check for $296.00 every month. I wanted that check, so I told Booger I would live with her. I knew that most of the time she was at work for a cleaning service or she was drunk, so how bad could it be?

I would find out.

Brendan, another kid Booger had taken in, told us how it

would be; he said we would become Booger's house niggas.

But my brothers and sisters and I moved in anyway. By this time, Shavonta had two babies. All of us got food stamps.

We had to serve Booger drinks. We had to fix her whatever she wanted, even if she was standing right there in the kitchen. She would curse us and say, "Y'all bad as hell. Y'all killed your mama and grandma. That's why they're dead. But you won't kill me."

Booger gave Curtis clothes for one month. Then everything stopped. I never saw my Social Security money; Booger took it all for herself.

I am not going to lie; one day we had a party at Booger's house while she was at work. But we had sense enough to get that house clean before she walked in the door. Booger came in and walked back out to a puddle at her front door step. It was full of red, muddy dirt. She stomped her feet in

> *"I never saw my Social Security money; Booger took it all for herself."*

that mud and walked through the house putting red dirt all over the carpet.

"Didn't I tell you motherfuckers to clean my damn house?" Booger yelled. She threw the clean dishes on the floor and broke some of them. She dumped the dish rack on the floor. She told Red, Curtis, Brendan and me to re-clean the house. Then she got her liquor, sat in her recliner, and watched TV while we cleaned.

That is the day Wookie left to go live with her boyfriend and his mama.

The first one of us Booger put out on the street was Shavonta. Shavonta had two kids; D'ajah was almost two and Demontray was two months. It was snowing. Shavonta asked for food stamps for her two babies.

Booger said, "You don't want to put food into my refrigerator. You get the fuck out of my house, you and your ugly-ass kids."

Shavonta said she would get Booger back. She did too. Shavonta put a Snickers bar in the gas tank of Booger's black Jeep Cherokee.

Shavonta moved in with a lady in the neighborhood.

A little later Booger put Red out too. So Red began sleeping in the park behind the church. He slept on the sliding board that had a red tunnel cover over it. We snuck Red in for baths and some food. Then a neighbor on 18th Street, Mrs. Williams, heard what was going on and took Red into her house. Mrs. Williams caught hell from Booger for taking Red in off the street.

But Mrs. Williams had rules at her house, and Red was not used to being told what to do. Red liked Mrs. Williams and her husband, Mr. Williams, but their world was not for him. After a while, Red was back on the streets.

That left Curtis and me at Booger's house. I asked Booger about the money from my check from my daddy. I was dressing like a rapper named Lil' Kim and wanted more clothes.

One day Booger was drinking her brown liquor. She looked at me and said, "I know you fucked my man. Every time you ask him to do something, he do it."

Booger's boyfriend said, "Booger leave that damn girl alone. We ain't doing shit. That just a child."

Booger told me to get the hell out of her house. I was fifteen years old when she put me out on the street.

> "I was fifteen years old when she put me out on the street."

MOTEL 6

27 My first night on the street, I dressed in the black dress with a pink daisy on the front that Ms. Palichat gave me four years ago. I put on the black tights and probably the same shoes too. The dress was shorter because I was getting taller, and my butt was growing.

I met up with Diamond (our arguments never lasted long) and the NCA on North Davidson Street. NCA stands for the North Charlotte Army; that is what we called our group of friends. We hung out, drank some beer, and smoked some weed. At one or two o'clock in the morning, everybody went home. I didn't tell anybody that I had gotten kicked out from Booger's house. I was a little high and felt ashamed that I had no place to live.

I walked down North Davidson Street. It was getting cold. It was dark. I knew crackheads would be looking for crack. A man pulled up in a black-on-black Mercedes. I was hungry, and I was tired. He asked me if I needed a ride. I said yeah. He asked where I wanted to go. I said, "Wherever you're going."

I told him that I had gotten kicked out of my house. He asked me if I was hungry. He took me to McDonalds. Then he took me to Motel 6 behind the McDonalds. He told me to go take a shower. I did, and then I put all of my clothes back on. I thought he was just being nice to me.

When I came out of the shower, he was naked on the bed. He told me to come to him. He was a big fat man. He rubbed me and asked me if I was okay. Then he did what he wanted to do. I lost my virginity that night.

After he was finished, I got up and went into the bathroom. It was different from all the times I had seen sex. I felt scared and confused. I felt like trash because I gave the man sex for food and a place to sleep. When I came out of the bathroom, there was $200 on the table by the bed. The man was gone. I took another shower and went to sleep.

The next day, I went to the front desk and said my "uncle" told me to pay for the room for the next two days. The room was already in the man's name, so I just needed to pay for more days. Nobody asked me questions; they just said okay. Then I went to buy some pads because I was bleeding, but I did not have my period.

I went to see Shavonta, who was living with a neighbor. I told her everything that happened. Shavonta was mad that Booger had put me out, but she was not surprised. "That damn Booger stupid as hell," Shavonta said.

She asked me where I slept. I told her a man had fed me and taken me to a hotel. Then Shavonta asked me what I did for that man to give me that meal and bed. I said, "What makes you think I did something?"

Shavonta said, "Anytime a man gives you something, they want something in return. So you lost your virginity?" I told her "Yeah, I guess so."

Then she told me to sell dope instead of my body.

> "Then she told me to sell dope instead of my body."

DEALING

28 Shavonta could get to all of her boyfriend Phazes' drugs and money. Phaze knew how to sell drugs, but he did not know how to manage the drug money. Phaze let Shavonta do that. He didn't know how much money went in and out.

Shavonta gave me some of Phazes' drugs and some of his money. She taught me how to set up a drug business. The first thing Shavonta said to me was, "Never get high on your own supply. Never."

And she told me never to take credit: "Make them pay when you serve them their drugs." Shavonta said to never trust a crackhead or junkie. A crackhead smokes a lot, but a junkie does nothing but smoke. They will do anything to get drugs.

Shavonta told me never to sell where I lay my own head. She said to go to the junkie or the crackhead in a crack house. A crackhouse is a junkie's house. The dealers we knew always paid the rent, so they could sell out of the house. Junkies can get power, water, gas, and everything else by stealing it and just need the dealer to pay the rent and give them drugs.

Shavonta showed me how to put powder cocaine, baking soda, and water in a jar and put the jar in a pot of boiling water. The cocaine and baking soda separate out and get solid when you add cold water or ice. Then you take the jar and shake it until the crack gets hard. You put the crack cocaine onto a brown paper bag to make it dry.

She showed me how to make a crack pack by putting the crack into sandwich bags, one dime in each corner.
A dime of crack is about the size of an apple seed.

A dealer starts by giving the junkie a "wake up." This is one dime of crack. Now the junkie is the slave of the dealer. The junkie will go to the homeless shelter and get all the other junkies who have lost everything to crack.

The junkies will steal and bring all kinds of stolen stuff to the dealers to get a dime of crack. Junkies will steal anything from cars to gold jewelry to Pampers diapers. Sometimes the junkies sell the stuff to someone in the 'hood for cash money. When I got my business going—got my foot in the streets—I would give a junkie a list of things I needed from the store, and he would steal it all and bring it back to me.

I lived in crack houses and would stay there all night if the business was booming. Business was fast because the junkies would buy dimes of crack, their highs would last about five minutes, and they would be right back for the next high. They have to be high all day.

A high crackhead or junkie is something to see. They climb the walls. They dig holes in their skin. They might jump out of a window. They are paranoid about the police. They think everyone (except for their dealers) is a cop.

Crackheads will do anything for crack. One time I saw a crackhead set himself on fire because the dealer told him to. Dealers like the power they have to make a crackhead do whatever they want him to do.

Homeless

29 I was living on the street, wherever I could sleep. Sometimes I went to the park behind the church. I would look to see if Red was sleeping on the sliding board with the red tunnel cover. If my brother wasn't there, it meant he was in jail or at some girl's house.

Sometimes I would head over to the jungle and wait until it was quiet, so I could sneak under the bridge to wash up in the creek. I always thought a crackhead was going to see me and rape me. I would stand in the cold water until it felt warm. I didn't have soap. I felt so dirty and just wanted to rinse off my legs, arms, and face at least. It was hard to sleep there though. You could hear dogs barking and their chains rattling all night.

When the sun came up, I would walk to a store and steal a toothbrush or deodorant. Then I would use a public bathroom to take a bird bath. I used paper towels and the hand soap that was in there. I used hand soap to brush my teeth too.

Sometimes I walked back to Caldwell Street. I would sit on the steps of the church and wait for Booger to go out. Then I would knock on the back window in the room where Brendan and Curtis slept. One of them would sneak me in the window, so I could find something to wear or something to eat. Booger still had all my clothes in her house and wouldn't let me get them. She was still getting my food stamps too.

THUG PASSION

30 Every day I woke up and had to find out where I would get money. I did one-night stands just to get somewhere inside to sleep and to get a bath and some money. I began to seduce guys from liquor and drug houses. But I was shy with men. That is why I took the drug ecstasy. It was a pill that put me in "thug passion mode."

Thug Passion was my street name. I made myself look like a ho, so I could feel like a ho. Ecstasy helped me become Thug Passion. When I was in Thug Passion mode, whatever I needed to get done would get done. I would steal, have sex with somebody, and sell drugs—whatever I had to do for the money.

I saw men give women ecstasy and get women drunk and have sex with them. So I started doing the same, luring men with ecstasy. I got the men drunk, and then I would kiss them with a Valium on my tongue to put them to sleep. The men thought the Valium was ecstasy. I watched them start to move in slow motion. When I saw their eyes close, I knew they were going off to another planet. Then I would rob them blind.

I thought I would never get caught. When I was high on drugs, I felt powerful and in control. I did not live for the future. I just tried to get through the day.

April 3, 2002

31 A couple of dealers I knew in the 'hood asked me if I wanted to make some money braiding their hair. I said that would be $40 ($20 a head), enough money to get a place to sleep that night.

I went with them to the hotel where they were living. There was a small kitchen in the room. We had picked up a frozen lasagna on the way there, and I said I would cook it for them.

Someone gave a knock on the door. There was another dealer in the room too. He opened the door and served a junkie his drugs. Then the junkie left.

I put the lasagna in the oven and started loosening one of the dealer's plaits to get ready to braid his hair.

Then there was another knock on the door.

This time there were three cops at the door. All of them were men. They looked around in the kitchen and found a big bag of crack. They found a shoebox full of money under the bed.

The cops started asking questions about where the drugs came from. But the three dealers just closed their eyes and ignored the cops. So now I'm thinking, "Damn! They're not gonna' tell the cops to let me go!"

One cop said to call a female officer. I was in handcuffs, and I was shaking. When I told the cop I was cold, he adjusted the air conditioner to make it colder.

The cops were saying things like, "We know y'all got more drugs. Where are the drugs?"

The dealers just said, "Man, we don't know what you talkin' about."

It took a long time for the female cop to get there. She uncuffed me, and we went in the bathroom. Then she said she had to search me. I told her I was on my menstrual.

The female cop asked, "How old are you?" I said I was sixteen.

She said, "Are you trying to be tough for these guys? If you are tough enough to hide drugs, you are tough enough to go to jail. You're going to jail with them."

I said, "I don't know nothin' about no drugs. I came up here to braid their hair and cook for them, so I could get some money for a hotel tonight."

When we came out the bathroom, the dealers were in cuffs and standing in line by the wall. The cops took all of us out to the cars waiting for us. I cussed at the dealer who was in the car with me for not taking up for me. The law of the street is if one person goes down, all go down, but the dealer could have told the cops that I was just there to braid hair.

At the police station, I got printed and got a mug shot. I had to take a shower with other women, and put on an orange jumpsuit that said Mecklenburg County Jail. I was downtown in the Fourth Street jail. There were people screaming and yelling.

My bond was set at $101,000. I got my one call, so I called Shavonta. She cussed me out and told me what to do. She said to wait until my court date: "And don't say shit to nobody."

I thought I could get out because I was a first time offender. But I was going to have jail time.

I had my own cell the first night. The lights were very bright. We had a buzzer to call the guard. I called the guard and said I wanted out of there. She told me to shut up and go to bed. Then the lights went out. It was pitch dark. I could not see one thing.

The mattress was about an inch thick. It was lumpy and it was green. At one end of the mattress was a hump for a pillow. It was hard.

There was yelling, and women were beating on the walls. I had heard about being raped in jail. I knew that if I showed weakness I would be used and abused. These people were like me . . . and worse. I was scared. I knew that if somebody tried to fight with me I might have to kill her.

I cried. I cried into that fake pillow for three hours straight.

I woke up early. I had no idea what time it was or what was going to happen next.

One jail mate came to me and said, "Everybody cries the first time in here." I didn't want any friends. I was just waiting for my court date.

Then they shipped me to

> "We had no identities except the ones we made day by day in the jail."

the Statesville jail, which was a lot bigger. I had shackles on my feet and handcuffs on my hands. Then they took me to the pod. It was huge. It had a top and bottom level, with cell after cell, and one big bathroom. They gave me a bucket with toothpaste, toothbrush, two pairs of socks, and some soap to take a bath and wash clothes. I was still on my menstrual with one pad. You had to buy your pads. I snuck tissue and hid it in my bucket of stuff.

The pod cells on the first and second floors were around the center where we ate. I did not eat anything. I did not drink anything. People in the jail said if you drank the "juice" they gave you, you would not be able to have babies.

I had a wristband with a number on it. We all got called by our numbers. We had no identities except the ones we made day by day in the jail. You had to be tough, or you would be someone's slave. You might have to do everybody's laundry—or do worse things.

I knew I could get hurt in this place, so I didn't sleep too hard. I used my socks to try and stay warm. The guards woke us up for a headcount at five or six o'clock every morning. We made our beds if we had covers. After we made our beds, we could not get under the covers until nine o'clock that night.

I was quiet. My face said: just try me, and I will whoop your ass. I braided other inmates' hair for soap or supplies. Braiding hair helped me get to know some inmates. I learned who to stay away from too.

There was one albino lady who was in for murder. Inmates told me to stay away from anybody in for murder because they were in for a long time. The murder thugs would try to mess you up if you were getting out soon. The albino had attacked inmates so they would get into trouble and have to stay in jail longer. You should never tell anybody what you were in jail for because they would know if you were getting out soon.

On the second or third day at Statesville, two inmates started talking to me. They were older ladies. One was called Wigger, for White Nigger, and the other was named Wendy. They told me to eat my food.

Wigger and Ms. Wendy were crackheads. They said that they remembered when they were young like me and just starting out with jail time. Ms. Wendy gave me a book about drug addiction with stories about heroin addicts. Even with everything I had seen in the crackhead jungle, those stories scared me.

Ms. Wendy said she had grandkids, but all she could think about was crack. She said to me, "You just a baby. You look like a six-year-old kid. I know I want crack more than I want my family. I wasn't always like that. I made that choice. What choice you gonna make, little girl?"

Wigger said, "I started out just like you—hangin' out with the dealers. I know I'll be back in here after I get out because crack is my life. I am proud to be a junkie. I will be one until the day I die. Is this what you want, baby girl? What you gonna do with your life?"

"If you come back in this jail," Ms. Wendy said, "we will act like we don't see you. You have a chance. But come back in here, you just like one of us."

I never thought I would be a crackhead. I hated crackheads. I used crackheads to make money. It scared me to hear Ms. Wendy talking about how she was just like me.

In the 'hood, I was in the drug world. I did not think about what would happen tomorrow; the only thing I thought about was how to protect myself and survive. But in jail, I did not have to worry about where I was going to sleep or what I was going to eat. Those two crackheads made me think. I thought about who I was and where I wanted to go.

I did not want to come back to jail. I did not want to be a crackhead only living to get crack.

I was in jail for one week and three days. The judge released me on an unsecured bond. I asked for a baloney and cheese sandwich before I left.

I forgot to give Ms. Wendy's book about the heroin addicts back to her, but I did not forget what she said to me.

> "People in the jail said if you drank the 'juice' they gave you, you would not be able to have babies."

MR. LAME

32 When Booger put me out, that left Curtis at Booger's house along with Brendan. Curtis and Brendan went to Teen Club at the church. All of their friends went there. It was a place to hang out after school. The club was in a separate house across the street from the main church building. Shavonta and I had gone to the club some, but by then we were street kids. The people who ran the club tried to help us, but we were not interested in their help and caused lots of trouble.

But when Curtis joined the club, there was a new director named Mr. Lame. At first, Curtis and Brendan liked Teen Club because Mr. Lame would make the girls do their homework but let the boys play. He let them watch movies and took them out to eat and let them play football. He told some of the boys to play outside; he kept some of the boys in his office.

Curtis told me that one day Mr. Lame grabbed Curtis by the belt buckle. He pulled Curtis toward him and said, "If you don't give it to me, I'm gonna take it." Curtis was scared and confused. Mr. Lame molested Curtis. Mr. Lame had molested Brendan too, but he was too scared and embarrassed to tell.

Curtis went to another adult who worked with the program and told him what Mr. Lame had done. The man said to write a statement and slide it under the door of the priest's office. Curtis did. The church got legal help. The case went to court, and the priest said he was sorry for the molestation. Everybody got paid not to say any more about Mr. Lame.

I was not surprised by this. To me, all of North Charlotte was the jungle, a place where people fought for money and their own survival.

> "... *but he was too scared and embarrassed to tell.*"

April 22, 2002

33 Shavonta and I were on Diamond's back porch, smoking a blunt.

We were telling Shavonta about the party last night and how this guy whispered in my ear, "I got $5,000 in my pocket. What you wanna do?" I told her how I just smiled and started pouring drinks from my mouth into his, feeding him liquor, until he was completely dysfunctional. Then I turned around and gave the guy a lap dance, leaning back and nibbling on his ear. The whole time I was going through his pockets and stuffing my bra with one hundred dollar bills. The dance lasted until there was no more money in his pockets. When I went to the bathroom to straighten the money, I counted $6,000. Then Diamond and I caught a cab back to the 'hood.

"Damn, bitch, now that's how you do it!" said Shavonta. We all laughed. And after that I went to a friend's house.

Maybe two or three hours later, Diamond was knocking on my friend's door, screaming. "Trina! Trina! Shavon not moving! Shavon not moving!"

I took off running down to Shavonta's house. There she was inside, lying on her back naked. Her two kids were on the bed crying. I checked her pulse. Shavonta was cold and stiff. The ambulance got there and said she was dead. It was a heart attack.

Shavonta was nineteen. My best friend, my sista and partner in crime. Dead.

Officer Linda

34 Officer Linda patrolled our 'hood and used to come around to see my brother Red. She tried to help him stay out of drug deals. She tried to help him stop training dogs to fight too. Officer Linda let my brother know that she wanted him to stay alive.

I liked Officer Linda, even though she was a cop. She drove a really huge pick-up truck. She had dark burgundy hair and wore blue mascara.

I was seventeen when Officer Linda asked me if I wanted a job. I told her sure. Officer Linda said I needed to get my Social Security card from Booger, so I could get a job. But Booger told me she did not have my card or my birth certificate; she said she lost them. I did not have any ID to say that I existed.

Officer Linda is about five feet two inches tall, but she is the type to keep on keepin' on. A lady at the Social Security office said that I needed two forms of ID to get a card. Officer Linda took me to the birth certificate office to get my birth certificate. She paid for it too. Then she told me to get a piece of mail from Booger's mailbox with my name on it.

With the birth certificate and the piece of mail, I had proof that I, Curtrina Pharr, existed. I got my Social Security card. Now I could get a job.

Officer Linda took me job hunting, but first we went to Taco Bell. We always got the same thing there: Mexican pizza and a large Mountain Dew. I had on a mini skirt and high heel shoes. I was dressed for the only type of job I knew: prostituting and selling drugs.

We went back to Motel 6 where I had been with my "uncle" when I was fifteen. Officer Linda got me a job in housekeeping.

At my new job, I had twenty minutes to clean each room. I went to work every day, but this was a crack hotel, and some of the rooms were torn up and nasty. I worked there for four or five months, but they let me go because they said I was too slow at cleaning. I just couldn't get some of those rooms cleaned in twenty minutes.

Officer Linda took me for my first haircut by a professional. I had a weave in my hair. One day, I asked Officer Linda to cut out the weave for me, and she cut off some of my real hair by mistake.

"Oh my God," she screamed. "I cut your real hair! You can hit me if you want."

"Nah," I laughed. "I can't hit no cop, especially a cop who is my friend."

But Officer Linda felt so bad about cutting my hair that she took me to a real stylist. I liked having my hair washed by somebody and having a towel wrapped around my head. The stylist cut my hair short with flips in the back and curls in the front. My bangs were raked to the side.

I felt beautiful.

DIAMOND'S MAMA

35 Officer Linda took me to the Department of Social Services. I told DSS that Booger was taking my check. I got a check from Social Security Administration from the legitimate work my father did while he was alive. But Booger was the payee, since I was still a minor. So Officer Linda had the idea of asking Diamond's mama if she would take custody of me. I had been calling her Mama for a while already.

I told Diamond and Mama that Booger kicked me out, but she was still getting my check from my father's Social Security. Diamond was still in high school. She said, "Fuck that bitch. Go back to school and get your check sent here to Mama, and Mama will give you your whole check."

Mama took me to Social Services. We signed paperwork, and she became my guardian. Living with her and Diamond was peaceful. Mama understood that I had been through a lot. She didn't fuss at me. She didn't hit me. She let me come and go as I pleased, but she put me in my place sometimes too.

Mama gave me my whole Social Security check. I still gave her some money for being able to live at her house. She did not ask me for a dime, but I wanted to help.

I used my money to buy a new bedroom suite for my very own bedroom at Mama's house. I was seventeen years old; this was the first time I had my own bed.

Officer Linda helped me get enrolled in Central Piedmont Community College (CPCC) in downtown Charlotte. I had dropped out of school in the eighth grade, so I needed to get my GED (General Equivalency Diploma) through CPCC.

> *"I was seventeen years old; this was the first time I had my own bed."*

MANN

36 I had a problem though. I was dating this guy named Mann. He was a drug dealer. Mann had been in and out of detention homes since he was fourteen. Mann did not want me to go back to school; he thought I would meet new people, which intimidated him. Mann wanted control over me and what I did.

One day, Diamond and I were standing with some other people at the bus stop at Elizabeth Avenue and Kings Drive, waiting for the bus to go home. It was lunch time. We saw the bus coming. I saw a brick-red Honda that looked like Mann's car next to the bus.

All of a sudden, Mann stopped his car and jumped out and ran in front of the city bus. He had rage on his face. He yelled at me, "You gonna stand here and talk to these niggas?" I froze. Mann grabbed my ponytail and pulled me to the ground by my hair. He started pulling me to his car by my hair and my shirt. He threw me into the car on the driver's side and kicked me to the passenger's side. I hid my face, and Mann pounded my head.

There were people changing classes. There were people in the bus watching all of this happen. There were people driving by in cars. Nobody stopped to help or call the police. I guess they were as scared as I was, but nobody helped me.

I did not go back to school for a while. I was scared and

embarrassed that Mann might show up again. I wanted to fit in, and the thought of Mann storming into a classroom scared me.

In the 'hood, you can feel like no one knows you exist. Since no one gets much attention, when someone does get noticed, people get jealous. I think that was Mann's problem. Diamond was like that too. Diamond got mad that Officer Linda was giving me so much attention and said she didn't want Officer Linda in her house any more. She started rumors in the 'hood that Miss Linda and I were lovers. But I still hung around with Officer Linda because I knew she cared about me. So Diamond told me to get out of her house.

I don't know why the 'hood is like that. I've seen some people try to change and fail. Then they use the failure as an excuse never to try again. And then some people never try at all, like they don't even know that change is an option.

> *" ... some people never try at all, like they don't even know that change is an option."*

Abandoned House

37 Officer Linda got me an apartment from one of her friends. The rent was $375 a month. My Social Security check stopped when I turned eighteen. I had to get money to pay rent. I was working at some jobs at temp agencies.

People in the 'hood started saying that I was snitching to Officer Linda. I got scared that they would try to hurt me. I started avoiding Officer Linda and did not want to let her in the apartment she had gotten for me.

I met this homeless girl who was living out of her car. She introduced me to Cupcake, who was a stripper. Cupcake had a pole in her house for pole dancing. She would throw a party and invite people who would pay for private dances and sex. Cupcake dressed me up for one of her parties. I was scared, so I took two shots of tequila. I wanted my rent money, so I danced hard. Money rained in on me.

I avoided drugs because I was scared of losing control of myself. I had learned a nasty lesson when I was drunk and Storm messed with me. And I remembered the things Wigger and Ms. Wendy told me in jail. Officer Linda did not know what I was doing to pay the rent. In my way, I was trying to do better by not taking drugs or selling drugs. But I was still selling my body.

I went back to what I knew and let people start snorting coke in my living room. I charged fifty dollars per person.

And like I said, I had sex to get money. A friend of mine took me to a house where there were lots of people. I walked into a room. My friend introduced me to a cop who was off duty. He and I had sex. The cop paid me $300.

Things got worse and worse. I took people into my apartment to make money. People were doing drugs. People lived with me, but no one paid any rent.

Then I met a real estate agent who said he would give me a house in trade for sex. The house had three bedrooms and was gorgeous, so I said okay and moved in my bedroom suite that I bought when I lived with Mama. Then he said he wanted some rent money too.

But he did not pay the mortgage, and the foreclosure notice came. The power got cut off. It was freezing cold and pitch black at night. Outside was cold; inside was even colder. I was alone and scared. One night I called Officer Linda because I couldn't get warm. She brought me a fur coat she bought from the mall.

The city hadn't turned off the water yet, but the showers were cold. I would wet a cloth, put soap on the cloth, and then wash up in the shower stall with the water off. I would turn the cold water on and turn around in circles three times to rinse off and then jump out. It was like showering in the snow.

But I kept living in the real estate man's abandoned house. When Granddaddy Pharr saw the house, he thought I had finally made it. He would stop by with a McDonald's hamburger sometimes to help me out. It was winter, and it was snowing. I went to work for some temp agencies to get some money.

I ate Slim Jims. I heated them with a candle or a lighter. I went to the CVS drugstore to charge my phone on the outside plug. I stole potato chips from the store to eat. I wore the same clothes all the time.

New Year's Eve night came. It was cold, and I was alone in the dark. There was no food. I lit a candle and started writing. I had to be real with myself. I was nineteen years old and had to get myself out of this mess.

I wrote this song and cried out the words; I had my arms stretched up to God.

> *My life has been so hard.*
> *I can't hide my faith, and I can't hide my scars.*
> *God said he wouldn't let it get this far.*
> *I've been reaching for you; could you grab my arms?*
> *You made a promise to me; I kept my faith,*
> *now I'm depending on thee.*
> **GOD, PLEASE HELP ME!**

ROCK

38 One afternoon a group of us went to Fayetteville to see Diamond's brother Kevin and some of his friends. Kevin was very smart. He had gone into the Air Force. We all started drinking and watching a boxing match on TV.

Somebody asked me where I came from and if I was a member of Kevin's family. I had been drinking, and when I drank I would tell my life story to get it out of me. I started telling them about my life and how Kevin's family had given me a place to live and food to eat. I told them I was three when my daddy died. I told them about my mama dying when I was eight and me going to live with my Grandma Nell and her dying too. I told them about moving in with my cousin Booger, until she put me out on the street. I told them about living in an abandoned house with no power or food. I did not tell them about the beatings; I thought they were just normal.

This guy at the party, one of Kevin's Air Force friends, came up to me. His name was Rock. He was a little guy with a high-pitched voice. Rock looked me straight in the face and said, "Don't nobody feel sorry for you. I had a hard life too. I grew up not far from you on Kenny Street, just around from Caldwell in North Charlotte. I got outta there. What you gonna do about it?"

I felt like I had been slapped. I looked at him and said, "You right. I am going to do something about it." Then he handed me a beer.

NET

39 I knew that I wanted to be like the people at the party. They were people who had done something with their lives.

I wanted to be like Diamond's sister, Net, too. She spoke educated and carried herself like a lady. Net had gone to Job Corps. She told me that Job Corps is the reason she carried herself so well. She got a great job and was a good mother.

Someone once told me people who just talk, talk forever; people who walk, they walk into success.

So I started walking.

I went to Mama. I told her that I was living in an abandoned house. My grandpa taught me never to ask for nothing. To ask showed that you were weak. So I didn't ask for help.

Mama said, "Baby, talk to me. What are you doing? How you eating?"

"I steal food. And Diamond gives me money," I said.

"What about no GED. You know I don't play that."

I told Mama I wanted to go to Job Corps to get my GED and make something of myself.

"Go get your stuff and move in here. That way you will have a place to live when you come back from Job Corps," she said.

Net warned me that the same mess that was going on in the 'hood was going on at Job Corps—sex, drugs, stealing. But the difference was at Job Corps you are on federal property. If you get caught there, you became a felon.

Another difference was you had food and a place to sleep. "You got clothes, and they give you some money," Net said. Not having to worry about where you were going to sleep, what you were going to eat, and how you were going to get money gave you time to do something to help yourself. She said it was a good program, and if you did right, you could learn a lot and move on with your life. I told her I wanted to start.

Net took me to sign up for Job Corps. She wanted me in a small program, so I would focus. I decided to enroll in the Lyndon B. Johnson Center in Franklin, North Carolina. I didn't know who Lyndon B. Johnson was.

My boyfriend encouraged me to go on to the Job Corps. He was sad to see me leave, but he knew I had to do something with my life. He gave me a gold cross with crushed diamonds and Jesus on the cross. He had bought it for a dime of crack, but to me that cross meant that I had protection. To leave everything I knew was scary. The cross made me feel like Jesus was with me.

Everybody else from the 'hood told me it was a waste of time for me to go to Job Corps. They said they went and did not finish, and I would do the same: "Girl you ain't gonna make it. You gonna get into trouble and hit some girl. You gonna fight up there."

They were like drowning people, and they wanted to make sure I went down too. It was like when I was in jail. The most dangerous convicts were the ones who were not getting out. They would do anything to keep you with them.

"They were like drowning people, and they wanted to make sure I went down too."

JOB CORPS

40 Net took me to the Greyhound bus station. Mama and Diamond cried their eyes out when I left. I was crying too because I did not know what to expect. But Net said not to worry. If she could do it, I could too. Net said to stay focused: "Do not mess with those girls up there. Be who you want to be. Focus on who you want to be."

Franklin is about 180 miles west of Charlotte. Except for the trip to Fayetteville where I met Rock, I had never been out of Charlotte. Rock's words were what started me on this journey. I had a gray cloth suitcase with all my clothes and six or seven pairs of shoes. I cared about my fashion look. I had my hair braided, so I would look good.

I sat in the back of the bus, so I could keep an eye on everything. I listened to music, so something I knew was with me. I looked at all the towns we drove through. The Job Corps program gave us a coupon for McDonalds, so we had something to eat.

When we got to the Lyndon B. Johnson Center, there was nothing but trees. Trees and lots of roads. I never saw so much space without buildings. I was scared. There was no place to hide.

When we got off the bus, we were put into groups of seven. There were rules about bathing and keeping clean. They told us to go for STD (sexually transmitted disease) tests. I was afraid of the STD tests because I had been prostituting.

Burning meant that you had a STD. But I wasn't burning, thank God.

Net had told me that the same crap that was on the streets was at Job Corps: drugs, gangs, and violence. I found out real quick that she was right. I let my group of seven know that I was no chap. I talked gangsta to my group; that was their language and what they understood.

"Y'all need to shut the fuck up. I want to listen to what these people have to say. We ain't been here a week, and y'all already getting trapped into this bullshit on campus," I said in a hardcore tone of voice. I did not want anybody messing with me.

Net had told me about the gang members and what they wore, and how they would try to get you to work with them instead of Job Corps. It was the same drama that was in the 'hood. Net told me to stay out of it and focus on what I could learn. I did that.

I made it clear that I would not tolerate any nonsense. I let them all know that I knew how to fight and would beat them if it came to that. Very fast I was respected as a leader. Even the gang leaders wanted me to be in their groups because their people looked up to me.

I told the gang leaders, "Do I look like I play games? Back off. I am here to learn something." I faced them straight on, no fear. They were not going to take this opportunity away from me. I remembered what Rock said. I saw who Net had become. I wanted a new life.

The Job Corps director noticed and said, "You look like a leader."

I became a bay leader. A bay leader is assigned to a hall; mine was Hall E. I had power over my group. I used that power to get them to want to do something with their lives. They became family. We had each other's backs. For the first time, I was a part of a group of people I could begin to trust and who were going in a positive direction.

We got up at six o'clock in the morning. We all wore uniforms. Net had not told me this; she knows how I love fashion, and there was nothing fashionable about the JC uniforms. We walked to the café and had a great breakfast that was made by the culinary students at Job Corps.

After breakfast, we went to the bus stop to be taken to Southwestern Community College in Franklin. The first person I met was my student counselor, Ms. Judy. I told her about everything about my life: the beatings, the homelessness, the drugs, and the prostitution.

She listened. Then she looked at me and said, "You've had a hard life. But it's up to you to make this work." That was it. I had poured out my guts, and I wanted some empathy. But Ms. Judy said the same thing to all the students: make it work.

Another student counselor was Mr. Paul. He really helped me because he listened. Then he got me to say what I wanted to do with my life. He kept encouraging me to keep my eye on the goal. He kept saying, "Why are you here?" I felt like I was an individual to him, not just another student.

Mr. Smith was my math teacher. My skills were about on the third grade level. Mr. Smith tried to push me. One day Mr. Smith yelled at me in the class. I waited until after class. I went up to him and told him not to yell at me in class. Mr. Smith told me I was the most mature student he had seen because I controlled myself when I was mad. He said other students might have thrown chairs in class and yelled back at him. He began to respect me, and I learned to respect him too.

Mrs. Rich was my writing teacher. She showed me her short stories. I sat near her desk. I did an essay on hurricane

Katrina. I started writing about my life in the 'hood in that class, but I was too shy to let anybody read it. I wrote "A Perfect Place" while I was at Job Corps:

> *There is a place with no sorrow*
> *There is a place for tomorrow*
> *There is a perfect place called heaven.*
> *There is a place where you can feel free*
> *There is a place for you and me*
> *There is a perfect place called heaven.*
> *When you need someone to talk to*
> *Call on the man who loves you*
> *This is a perfect place called heaven.*
> *When you call the name Jesus*
> *His holiness will feed us*
> *This is a perfect place called heaven.*
> *When you show that you are righteous*
> *His blessings are priceless*
> *This is a perfect place called heaven.*
> *For those who really care*
> *I would like to share*
> *He won't put any more on you than you can bear*
> *This is a perfect place called heaven.*

I was determined to make Job Corps work for me because I had seen how other peoples' lives had gotten better. When I looked in the mirror, I wanted to see someone I liked. Nothing could hurt me any more than life had already hurt me. I knew how to play the street game, but I wanted to win at this new game.

Job Corps gave me the structure I never had. We were up early every day. We went to school one week and then trade school the next week.

There was one technology teacher who was really strict. She made me feel like she really cared about me because she took time to work with me individually. Because she took interest in me, I tried harder. I stopped playing on the computer and started trying to do my work the right way. I was intimidated by her and wanted her respect. She gave me respect by having high expectations of me. She said she knew I could do the work. On the last day of class, I got a hug from her.

I became the student government association representative. I took the meeting notes and gave students advice. I was a leader in the 'hood because I could fight; I was a leader at Job Corps because I was serious about my work and my peers. I didn't like slackers, and I didn't deal with them unless they showed me that they wanted something for themselves.

This was a hard group to lead. Some psycho cases were there. One kid would start yelling, "One, two, I gonna kill all of you." The staff turned to the leaders in the group like me to handle the kids. I used my street smarts when I needed to, but lots of times just listening and talking with respect to the group got things calmed down. It had worked with me, so I used the tough respect with the others in the group.

But when we went to Virginia on a field trip, I went back into my old survival mode. In survival mode, I got what I needed or wanted any way I could. I saw some clothes I wanted in a mall in Virginia, and I stole them.

I had gained weight at Job Corps, and my clothes were small. I wanted to look stylish when we were not on campus. Job Corps paid us a basic living allowance of fourteen dollars every two weeks, but I spent that on hygiene and cosmetic items. I didn't have money for new clothes.

I made what I did okay in my mind because I had no family, no money, and needed the clothes. One of the JC students almost caught me stealing shoes. She crept up behind me trying to scare me in the shoe store. I had just taken off my old shoes; I put on the new pair and put my old pair in the shoe box. She didn't notice. I was the leader and didn't want her to pick up some of my bad habits. I didn't want her to get caught doing something that I taught her. That is not something that leaders do. I was more worried about her getting caught than I was about me getting caught.

When we got back to the Job Corps center, one of the students told me that in Virginia you could hang for stealing. She said, "They hang your ass up here." I did not want to get caught and kill my chances to get further along with my life.

When I was safe back at Job Corps with everything I needed, I was out of survival mode. I could think clearly. I knew I was gambling with everything I had worked for. So that was it. That was the last time I ever stole.

I felt important at Job Corps. People looked up to me. People came to me for advice. For the first time in my life, I felt like I was somebody, not because people were afraid of me but because people respected me. I was respected for my abilities in school and for my abilities helping people. I wanted to be different from who I had been, different from other chaps off track. I was learning to respect myself for being strong and taking the high road.

I was at Job Corps for six months. I got my GED. The sooner you improved and learned a new way to live, the sooner you could leave. But I was scared to leave. I felt as scared leaving as I had coming. Where was I going next? Job Corps gave me a transition person to help me find my way.

The day I graduated was the greatest day of my life. I smiled as big as I could. I was proud of me. I had no family there, but I did not need them, because I was so thankful to be who I was. I was someone I respected.

> *"For the first time in my life, I felt like I was somebody, not because people were afraid of me but because people respected me."*

BEAUTIFUL DISASTER

41 When I got back to Charlotte, I moved back in with Diamond and Mama. I got a job with CVS Pharmacy. The manager of the CVS asked me if I ever had a job in customer service. I said, "No, because nobody ever gave me a chance." He said, "Today is your chance." I became the photo lab tech and customer service representative.

CVS paid me seven dollars and twenty-five cents an hour. The manager paired me with a positive girl named Jade who trained me on the job. Jade was going to college. She talked to me about setting goals.

I had been at CVS for a year and a half when this customer came in and said she liked the way I worked. She asked me if I would like a job at Carolinas Medical Center (CMC) in the Sterile

"Everyone said I would fail. My friends said they did not like my new attitude. I felt alone."

Processing Distribution Department. The job paid ten dollars and twenty-five cents an hour. I interviewed for the job and got it.

But it was hard living in the 'hood. None of my family wanted me. Everyone said I would fail. My friends said they did not like my new attitude. I felt alone.

Even my best friend, Diamond, said that I talked like a white person. "I don't even know who you is anymore. You got some kind of new values. You even listen to cracker music and all that shit."

One of the songs I liked to listen to was Kelly Clarkson's "Beautiful Disaster." The song is about something that is beautiful on the outside but a disaster on the inside. It reminded me of my relationship with Mann. From the outside looking in, our relationship was perfect. We looked good together, and he bought me nice things. But behind closed doors, he was physically abusive. I knew I couldn't be with someone who would beat on me from out of the blue.

I tried to let all the negative talk roll off my back. But I wanted an apartment out of the 'hood. I had to get out of where I had learned my past behavior. I had to be in a new place. My time with Diamond and Mama was a wrap. It was time for me to move on.

I would have to show people that I could make it, not just talk the talk. I felt bad about leaving everybody I knew, but I guess that is what walkers do.

> *"I don't even know who you is anymore. You got some kind of new values."*

DWANE

42 I went back to survival mode. I did what I knew how to do: I sold drugs and went back to prostituting to get enough money for an apartment. But I prostituted only on the weekends, so I could still show up for work at CMC.

I moved to a two-bedroom house on Ross Avenue off of West Boulevard. It was bluish green with a porch. The front window was made of glass brick, so I did not have to buy a curtain. The driveway was paved. It had a yard with grass and a big tree in the front.

But there was no gate in the backyard fence. Crackheads would walk by and say, "Girl you need to let me cut your grass." The only way to get to the backyard was to come through the house. They would have to walk through the house with the lawnmower. I did not want crackheads in my house, so I asked the landlord to put a gate in the fence. But he wouldn't.

I had a new boyfriend named Dwane. He was funny and laid-back. He was the second boyfriend who didn't hit me. He helped support me financially. I lived alone on Ross Avenue, but Dwane came over every day for sex and to take me to work at Carolinas Medical Center.

Dwane gave me money, but he was not faithful to me; he was always in the street looking for hos. Dwane was a common lady's man. He worked at night as a janitor. Other than chasing skirts, he was a good man to me.

I lived in the house on Ross Avenue for six months. But then I got fed up with the landlord and moved to a one-bedroom apartment at Forest Brook apartments.

I still felt lonely and scared. One day I prayed to God and asked Him to send me someone to be with me.

I started having panic attacks. I felt like I was going to die. I called Diamond. The first thing she asked me was about my period. Diamond asked Mama to get a pregnancy test. They gave me the test. It was positive.

Mama was excited that I was having a baby. I was shocked. I didn't know what to do.

I developed gallstones. I was confused about what was happening with my body. I was in and out of the hospital. My manager at CMC got fed up with me calling out for panic attacks. I lost my job when I was a little more than two months pregnant.

> *"I still felt lonely and scared. One day I prayed to God and asked Him to send me someone to be with me."*

JUNE 30, 2009

43 Dwane Jaquice Pharr was born. He weighed eight pounds three ounces and was twenty-six inches long.

The best day of my life was graduating from Job Corps because that was the day the new me was born. But the day Dwane was born was the second best day of my life. My first words to my son were, "Happy Birthday. I love you. I am going to do my best."

Some of my family came to the hospital to see my baby. Booger came to see me too. But she would not let the daddy, Dwane, in the delivery room while she was there. She said, "You need to go ahead and give me this baby." I knew she just wanted my baby for the food stamps and other benefits.

When I woke up the first full day of my baby's life, I felt like it was Christmas because I had something waiting for me. I felt real love. I wanted to be a good mama for my son.

I had a C-section, so I stayed in the hospital until July 4—freedom day. Little Dwane won best dressed at the hospital. I took him home to my apartment that night.

There was an eviction notice in my mailbox.

I was scared the first night with my baby. I never had taken care of a baby before. His daddy came over at three o'clock in the morning high. The next day, Dwane said he could not pay the rent. Another girl was having his baby too.

I needed a place for my newborn baby boy and me to live.

SURVIVAL

44 I called my brother Curtis's baby's mama, and we moved to an apartment with her and her children.

I took little Dwane to the doctor for everything. Most of the time there was nothing wrong with him. No one told me my boy was going to change colors right before my eyes. Hell! It scared me half to death! But the doctor was polite and said very kindly, "He is changing into his natural color, which is African American." I laughed the whole way home.

I became a private dancer and went back to prostituting to pay the bills. I paid my little cousin to keep Dwane. When I got a call from a prostitution client, I would go to hotels, mansions, suites at the Hilton—wherever they were. I had clients who were lawyers, businessmen, police officers, realtors, an accountant, and a doctor. Most of them were married. I did what they wanted me to do and listened to them fuss about their jobs or their wives. It took about fifteen or twenty minutes to do the job. I got $250 per person. If they were from out of town and wanted more time with me, I charged $400.

But I knew this wasn't what I wanted to do with my life.

I went to Social Services to apply for a Work First check. They assigned me to an employment worker. She gave me an application for childcare resources. She said the wait for childcare could be five to six years or longer.

There were so many people looking for benefits in the social work government office. I knew the social workers thought we were all lazy and not wanting to better ourselves. I was not like that, and I wanted to show the social workers that I wanted to work and be somebody. I had hit rock bottom hard, this time with a child to take care of. I could only look up. There was no bottom left.

When I got to my employment worker, I said, "I know your job is overwhelming. But I am not like all the people in here. I have a plan."

She was older lady with glasses. She looked at me and leaned back. She had a smirk on her face and said, "Oh really. What's your plan?"

"I am a single mother. I have no parents. I don't have nobody to take care of my child. It is only me and my son. I need my child in daycare, so I can make moves. I am going back to college. I am going to find a part time job. I am going to find us a place to live."

She said, "I believe you." She put my application for childcare on the top of a huge pile.

I said, "Hold on. I'm gonna put a star on it." We laughed. I got a letter in three weeks saying that I was approved for childcare.

> "I am a single mother. I have no parents. I don't have nobody to take care of my child. It is only me and my son. I need my child in daycare, so I can make moves."

GOD

45 I learned how to do job searches on the computer through the Work First program. But in between jobs, I was still stripping to make ends meet.

Dwane's daddy bought Pampers. He said we could live with him if I let him have other girls. But I wanted more than that for little Dwane and me.

My son and I went from place to place for almost two years. My sister Wookie said I could live with her and her four children. Dwane and I slept on the floor because it was so crowded there.

It seemed like the devil was always trying to pull me down. But lil' Dwane was always taken care of. I paid bills wherever we went.

When I was twenty-five years old, I fell to my knees and prayed. I thanked God for protecting my son and me on our journey. Then I made a vow to Him that I would never strip or sell my body again. A week later things fell into place: I got an apartment and a job, and a friend loaned me a car to get to work. A year later, I've kept my promise to God, and He continues to answer my prayers.

LESSONS LEARNED

46 After all our struggles comes a time to where we can look at our past and be bitter, or we can capture the lessons. To follow are my summaries of gratitude.

MISS TRINA

 Today I live in a subsidized housing community in Charlotte with about fifty apartments. Having a job helped move me up on the five-year waiting list.

Little Dwane is four years and goes to Head Start. He is smart and happy. I want my child's life to be better than mine was. I set goals for my son. I have a plan to get my child where I want him to be, a plan for where I want to be.

Lil' Dwane makes me smile more. His daddy comes to pick him up every Saturday, and they hang out together for the weekend. Lil' Dwane adores his daddy.

My son helped me to overcome being afraid to voice my opinion because I have to make decisions for him and make sure that they're the right decisions. He helped me become a powerful person that I didn't know existed. I thank God everyday for him.

I am a full-time student majoring in English at Central Piedmont Community College. I want to get a bachelor's degree in film production. I just graduated from bartending school too. My plan is to spend my weekdays going to school and taking care of little Dwane. I will bartend on the weekends while he is with his daddy. For now, I work in retail to pay the bills.

I am getting closer and closer to where I need to be in life. My neighbors call me Miss Trina. They respect me. They say they notice the way I treat my son. I spend time with him. I do not yell at him or use words I do not want him to use.

I do not judge them for living the way they do. I have been where they are. People who spent time with me and did not judge me helped me to change.

I listen to my neighbors when they need to get things off their chest. We talk about our stories.

Living in the ghetto, you hear and see a lot of things. Most of our stories are about child abuse and child molestation. We come from families with alcoholism, drug addiction, and incarcerated parents. One thing we all have in common is that we were left astray with not even a clue of what steps we needed to take to begin fitting into a normal world.

But just because you live in the 'hood doesn't mean you have to be like the 'hood. I tell these women that there is a way out. I show interest in their futures.

Sometimes my neighbors ask me for advice. I'm a positive voice that my peers need to hear. God is using me to be the voice for the people who are only noticed when something goes bad.

Little Dwane and I pray together, and we go to St. Paul Baptist Church every Sunday. It keeps me closer to God, so I'll never get the urge to stray away from Jesus again. It feels a lot safer to walk with Christ.

My past is not my excuse; my past is my motivation. I know where I have been, but only God knows where I am going.

MAMA

● My mama did a lot of wrong things as a parent; however, I am thankful for her bringing me into the world. If I hadn't seen my mother struggle to provide for her five children alone, I would probably be in her very same situation. They say some people learn faster than others. I learned the responsibilities of an adult a lot faster than most people my age because my mother didn't hide anything from us. With that being said, I learned very quickly after Dwane was born that one child is hard to raise, so my mother definitely had it hard with five children. I also learned that life is about choices. My mother chose to have unprotected sex with our fathers. Now that I'm grown, I also know that mistakes can happen, but she also chose to party all the time. I on the other hand, choose to be responsible with the choices I make. I choose to finish college and get married before I have any more children. I work hard at everything I do with hopes that it will someday pay off. My son admires me, and I really want him to be proud of me some day.

Nell

● Nell didn't like showing emotion or any kind of affection. She never played with us, she was firm, and she only gave out hugs and said I love you when she was drunk. When she gave orders, she only wanted to say things once. Nell was what you call "old school." She lived by the saying, "I'm grown; stay in a chap's place," meaning she could say and do as she pleased but better not catch her grandkids saying or doing anything we saw adults do. Nell taught us discipline and structure like cleaning up behind ourselves and respecting adults. Nell made having five kids look easy. We never went hungry or ran out of soap and tissue. She loved us, but she was too hardcore to be as affectionate as Rudy's parents were on *The Cosby Show*. I believe the verbal and physical abuse was from the way she may have been treated as a child; nevertheless, Nell was so skinny we barely felt the whoopins most of the time. I even remember my brother and me hiding under her blanket while she tried to whoop us with a switch. We were laughing so hard she actually thought we were crying. It was even funnier when she was drunk. Nell's whoopins where a piece of cake compared to Mama's, except one day when Nell beat us with a Nerf-like bat for jumping out of our two-story apartment window while she was asleep. Red and I decided to act like our apartment was on fire and jumped out of the top window over and over again, not to mention we pushed Curtis out of the window, but he didn't land right, so we didn't let him play anymore. We actually deserved a butt whoopin' that day but not with a bat.

> "We never went hungry or ran out of soap and tissue. She loved us, but she was too hardcore to be as affectionate as Rudy's parents were on The Cosby Show."

BOOGER

● Booger taught me a valuable lesson in life. I learned that trust is not a gift. You really have to be careful whom you allow to sit around you and your kids. My mother and my grandmother trusted Booger, and so did I. Writing this book helped me realize that she was always in the center of all the drama between family and Social Services. When she finally got what she wanted and saw that we weren't receiving a large amount of Social Security income like she had been thinking all of these years, she threw us out like trash. She had a job, a house, and a car, but she wasn't satisfied. She envied my mother and grandmother for so many years, and she always found a way back into their lives by saying things like, "We're family," "I love y'all," and "I miss the kids," and Mama and Nell fell for it every time.

When I birthed my son and we hit rock bottom, guess who called Social Services on me. You guessed it—Booger! And she also tried to use the family card to get back in our lives. Well,

> *"I learned that trust is not a gift. You really have to be careful whom you allow to sit around you and your kids."*

her family card has been declined for a few years now. Booger didn't even bother teaching us to be independent like she was. If she took us in for the right reasons and showed us how to get jobs, cars, and houses like she had, then every child she ever had in her custody would love and respect her to this day. Instead, we all grew up and chose to live our lives without her.

I forgive Booger because her childhood was terrible, but I choose to love her from a distance. People as broken as Booger need time to themselves to heal from the inside out. Her problems are deep to the core, but obviously she could have chosen to be different from family, like I did. I don't believe in excuses. I pray that she heals because I know what it feels like to be trapped inside the person you hate the most. I let all of the hate and anger go in this book, so I could live and be happy. I feel free now, and it feels awesome!

> *"I forgive Booger because her childhood was terrible, but I choose to love her from a distance."*

SHAVONTA

● Shavonta was more than my sister; she was my best friend. She showed me in so many ways how much she loved me. One thing I can say about my sisters and brothers is that we all stuck by each other through our struggle. Shavonta gave me weed and alcohol to get me to sit down and listen to her lectures about the bad choices I was making. Barely more than a child herself and a product of the 'hood, she saw supervising my high as a nurturing act and a way to get my attention. I believe she knew I was following behind her, so she must have felt obligated to teach me personally how to be smart on the streets and most importantly to be safe. Shavonta taught me how to sell drugs instead of my body. Now that I'm an adult, I interpret that lesson a lot differently. I think Shavonta was trying to teach me how to earn money without the risk of catching HIV or being beaten or raped. She knew what it was to be beaten and raped. She cared more about the four of us than she cared about herself. She was tough; I wish she was still here. Truthfully, I would have been whatever she turned out to be. I remember being furious with God because he didn't take me instead. I felt like I needed her around because I didn't know how to act without her. I needed a leader. She used to say, "What the hell is a good life anyway?! Trina, do you see anybody happy to see us? We all we got! Life is a bitch, and you better know she ain't giving us shit." Shavonta was right. Ain't nobody ever gave me nothing. I've always had to do something in order to receive something. When someone offers you something, remember nothing in life is free. Know what you're getting yourself into.

"Shavonta was more than my sister; she was my best friend."

RED

● Red showed me hard love growing up. He has always been the man of our family. Whenever he saw me talking to boys or smoking and drinking, he would mug me in the face and push me all the way home. He was so mean growing up; I literally used to run from him. He was trying to teach me to have self-respect. The way I was dressing and partying with guys made him feel like I was being promiscuous. He was right; I was. I was trying to grow up too fast and really wasn't ready for that. I was attracting the wrong attention from adult men. I was copying my sister and my aunt Dor'ann. They made everything they did look sexy. My brother didn't want me to be like that. I don't remember not one person in our family admiring anything he did. He was constantly beaten and verbally abused as a child. He had it harder than I did. So did Shavonta. I think he bullied me to get his point across the way people in the family bullied him. He was so young, and not one person in the family acknowledged the good in him. His father didn't even want him. That is a lot to hold in, especially as a child but even as an adult. We are now closer than my other sister and brother. I appreciate his lesson. I carry myself like a queen now, a feisty one. I don't trust a man as far as I can throw them. Who knows—maybe someday that will change.

MANN

● Mann and I were perfect for one another at first. We had the same struggle in life. We understood each other; however, when love became domestically violent, verbally and physically, I knew it was time to end our relationship. When love gets physically and emotionally abusive, the best thing to do is love that person from a distance. It's going to take more than you to help the person you love realize that abuse is not a method of love. I loved Mann enough to leave him, so he could figure out what love actually was. I had hope that he would someday find himself under all of the gold teeth and gangsta life style.

I struggled with relationships because I always wanted to fill the void of losing my father. I lost my father before he got the chance to have "the talk" with me. No one told me to never let a man beat me. No one explained to me that some men will use you for sex and even abuse you before or after

> *"When love gets physically and emotionally abusive, the best thing to do is love that person from a distance."*

sex. No one told me that a man isn't supposed to cage you like an animal or question your every move like a criminal on parole. That negative behavior was all I saw.

Never let a man validate who you are or what you can do with your life. You never know—he could be hating on you secretly because he knows he doesn't have a chance in hell at succeeding in life, while you do. Don't listen too closely to the "I love yous" unless someone's actions show you the love is true. Don't settle. Be with the individual who is best for you. I am currently still single because now that I know better, I'll do better!

> *"No one told me that a man isn't supposed to cage you like an animal or question your every move like a criminal on parole."*

DIAMOND

● Diamond was a cool friend to have as a child. She inspired me to want an education. Diamond always spoke about becoming a lawyer or a mortician. I had no idea what I wanted to be, but thanks to Diamond I knew I wanted an education. Diamond was smart, popular, and funny. She was a leader. She always made sure her work was done and never missed school. I learned from Diamond that in order to be successful in life you have to show up and do your best. She taught me to never make fun my priority because it is my reward. In other words, work first and party later. I use this lesson in my every-day life.

> *"I learned from Diamond that in order to be successful in life you have to show up and do your best."*

OFFICER LINDA

● Officer Linda was a blessing in my life. She really showed me a different way to live. She began showing me herself how to fit into a normal society by showing me how to get a job and take care of myself. She got me an apartment, so I wouldn't be sleeping with men and staying in abusive relationships just to have a place to live. She talked to me about school and how we had some things in common and how she rose above her circumstances and is clearly successful. She is an unbelievable woman. She was my beginning to normalcy and adjusting to becoming myself, which is a civilized American citizen. She saw potential in me that I didn't see. She had patience with me. She actually took time out of her busy schedule to straighten me out. And she did it with class. She didn't beat me; she didn't question my life style; and she went in with an open mind and heart. And, Miss Linda, it paid off. Who knew that I would get help from the Charlotte-Mecklenburg Police Department? We had a lot of fun together. We gave Christmas gifts out of her trunk one year. I felt so great about that. Thank you, Officer Linda. You mean a great deal to me!

ROCK

● Rock was an individual I met briefly in Fayetteville. I didn't know him prior to that meeting and have not seen or heard from him since. Rock played a big part in my first step toward change. Had I not gone on that trip, I may have taken longer to realize I was using my circumstances as an excuse to fail. I sat at that fire and poured all of my problems out on a group of strangers, and Rock looked me dead in my face after twenty or thirty minutes of listening to me talk and said, "So. Don't nobody feel sorry for you. What are you going to do about it?" I felt offended and grateful all at the same time. I honestly didn't know whether to smack him or hug him because I knew that he was keeping it real. Rock shared with me that we were from the same 'hood, except he made necessary steps to remove himself from the world he grew out

"Sometimes it takes a person ignoring your feelings and telling you the truth for you to acknowledge your weaknesses."

of. Sometimes it takes a person ignoring your feelings and telling you the truth for you to acknowledge your weaknesses. This type of advice is supposed to come from friends and family; however, my lesson came from a stranger. God sends people your way for a reason. Imagine if I would have reacted negatively; I would have missed the importance of his statement, which was nobody owes me anything.

I have to work hard like everyone else. That is the message I got from Rock that night. For that, Rock, I am forever thankful. Thank you for being real with me. Thanks for not sparing my feelings because that's exactly what I needed. I hope you are still staying positive and are super-successful by now. With the ambition you had back then, I'm confident that you are doing big things now. Stay blessed, and most importantly, stay you.

"... I was using my circumstances as an excuse to fail."

AFTERWARD

● Curtrina Pharr and Catherine Fleming met in 1995 when Curtrina lived with her grandmother, Nell, on Caldwell Street. Curtrina was ten years old. Her mother had died the year before.

Catherine was working with the Seeds of Hope program sponsored by Christ Episcopal Church in Charlotte, North Carolina. Seeds of Hope was a group of fourteen programs in Charlotte's inner city. Catherine was a part of the Health in Partnership program that worked with families to improve health practices and access to health care and medications.

The Seeds of Hope/Health in Partnership grant was a five-year program. Catherine got to know all the Pharr children, especially Curtrina and Red. Curtrina had been taught not to ask for help; she was taught to survive on her own. But she and Catherine developed a friendship.

Curtrina was fifteen when she was kicked out of Booger's house. The Seeds of Hope program ended, and Catherine did not know what had become of Curtrina. Catherine had heard that Curtrina was living with a drug dealer who was beating her.

In 2012, Catherine was having lunch with Linda Williams, a community activist in the Optimist Park neighborhood where Curtrina had lived. (Throughout the book, Curtrina refers to this Linda as Mrs. Williams, so as not to confuse her with Officer Linda.) Catherine and Linda had met when

Linda ran the after-school program at the church in Nell's neighborhood. Linda had taken Curtrina's brother Red into her home for a while. Catherine asked if Linda knew where Curtrina was. Linda said, "Curtrina is doing well. She has a son. She is not taking drugs. She may still party some, but all in all, she is a good mother."

Linda sent Curtrina an email, and Curtrina immediately messaged Catherine on Facebook: "Oh my God, Miss Catherine! You were the only bright spot in my life. I have been looking for you. I would like to see you."

Catherine called Curtrina. They met at Curtrina's apartment and talked for two hours. Catherine told Curtrina about her own life: her father's suicide when she was ten years old and her mother's alcoholism.

Curtrina said, "I had no idea. You hid it so well."

"I didn't hide it. I was working on accepting it," said Catherine. "I could relate to your feelings of abandonment—not being sure where your parents were."

"Yeah, I used to wonder, 'Why me, Lord?'" said Curtrina.

"Me too!" Catherine laughed. "I'm white. I'm twice your age. I've had economic advantages. But I still felt just like you did. I felt like I wanted to live my life differently from the lives some of my family members were living. I had to build myself back up, just like you have."

"Miss Catherine, I have a journal," said Curtrina. "Would you like to read it?"

And from that journal came *Confessions of an Abandoned Child*, Curtrina Pharr's story of struggle, survival, and hope.

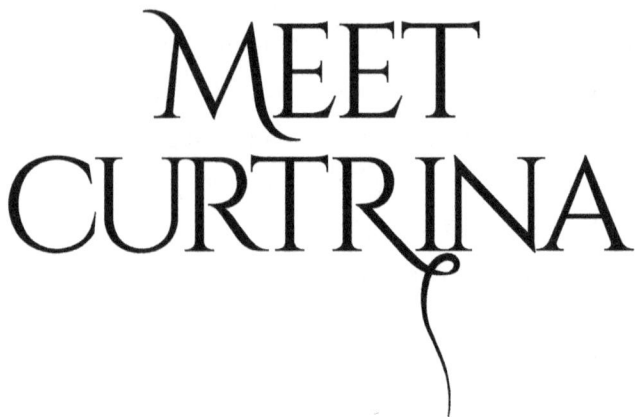

MEET CURTRINA

This book was written and produced to share this story and to change lives. Visit **curtrinaprojects.com** to invite Curtrina Pharr speak to your organization and to purchase additional copies of the book to share.

www.ingramcontent.com/pod-product-compliance
Lightning Source LLC
Chambersburg PA
CBHW070547090426
42735CB00013B/3099